LANDMARKS OF

# AMERICAN WOMEN'S HISTORY

James Oliver Horton
General Editor

# LANDMARKS OF
# AMERICAN WOMEN'S HISTORY

# Page Putnam Miller

UNIVERSITY PRESS

Published in consultation with the
National Register of Historic Places, National Park Service, the National Park Foundation
and the Gilder Lehrman Institute of American History

*In memory of my mother, Dorothy Page Putnam*

# OXFORD
UNIVERSITY PRESS

Oxford   New York
Auckland   Bangkok   Buenos Aires   Cape Town   Chennai
Dar es Salaam   Delhi   Hong Kong   Istanbul   Karachi   Kolkata
Kuala Lumpur   Madrid   Melbourne   Mexico City   Mumbai   Nairobi
São Paulo   Shanghai   Singapore   Taipei   Tokyo   Toronto

Published by Oxford University Press, Inc.
198 Madison Avenue, New York, New York, 10016
http://www.oup-usa.org

Oxford is a registered trademark of Oxford University Press

Library of Congress Cataloging-in-Publication Data

Miller, Page Putnam
  Landmarks of American women's history / Page Putnam Miller.
      p. cm. — (American landmarks)
"Published in association with the National Register of Historic Places,
National Park Service, and the National Parks Foundation."
Includes bibliographical references and index.
  ISBN 0-19-514501-1 (alk. paper)
1.  Historic sites—United States. 2.  Historic buildings—United States.
3.  Women—United States—History. 4.  Women—Monuments—United States.
5.  United States—History, Local. 6.  United States—Antiquities. I. Title.
II. American landmarks (Oxford University Press)
  E159.M557 2003
  973'.082—dc22                                          2003015341

Printing number:  9 8 7 6 5 4 3 2 1

Printed in Hong Kong on acid-free paper

Cover: *As dean and president of Bryn Mawr College, M. Carey Thomas (inset) built a library as grand as at any men's school of the time.*

Frontispiece: *Mary Chase Perry sits at a potter's wheel in her studio at Pewabic Pottery in Detroit, Michigan.*

Title page: *The first International Convention of Women, organized by Elizabeth Cady Stanton and Susan B. Anthony in 1888.*

JAMES OLIVER HORTON
General Editor

*Landmarks of African-American History*
*Landmarks of American Immigration*
*Landmarks of American Indian History*
*Landmarks of American Literature*
*Landmarks of the American Presidents*
*Landmarks of American Religion*
*Landmarks of the American Revolution*
*Landmarks of American Science & Technology*
*Landmarks of American Sports*
*Landmarks of American Women's History*
*Landmarks of the Civil War*
*Landmarks of Liberty*
*Landmarks of the Old South*

# LANDMARKS OF
# American Women's History

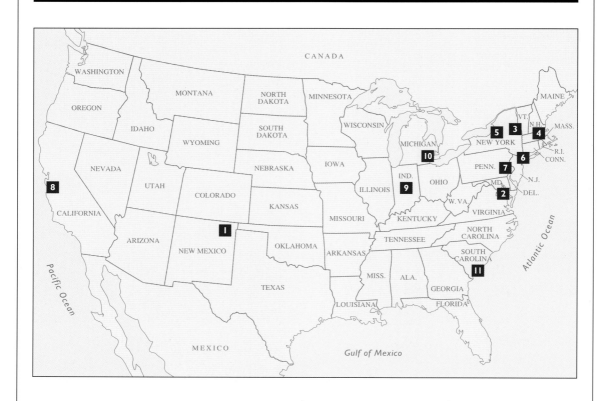

# Contents

Page 14
Taos Pueblo

Page 79
M. Carey Thomas Library

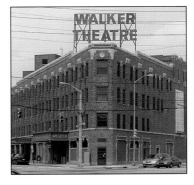

Page 102
Madam C. J. Walker Building

# Introduction:
# The Power of Place

*James Oliver Horton*

*General Editor*

Few experiences can connect us with our past more completely than walking the ground where our history happened. The landmarks of American history have a vital role to play in helping us to understand our past, because they are its physical evidence. The sensory experience of a place can help us to reconstruct historical events, just as archaeologists reconstruct vanished civilizations. It can also inspire us to empathize with those who came before us. A place can take hold of us, body, mind, and spirit. As philosophers of the Crow Indian nation have reminded us, "The ground on which we stand is sacred ground. It is the blood of our ancestors." It is the history owed to our children. They will remember that history only to the extent that we preserve the places where it was made.

Historical sites are some of history's best teachers. In the early 1970s, when I was a graduate student in Boston, working on a study of the nineteenth-century black community of that city, I walked the streets of Beacon Hill imagining the daily lives of those who lived there a century before. Although I had learned much about the people of that community from their newspapers and pamphlets, from their personal letters and official records, nothing put me in touch with their lives and their time like standing in the places where they had stood and exploring the neighborhood where they lived.

I remember walking along Myrtle Street just down Beacon Hill from the rear of the Massachusetts State House in the early morning and realizing that Leonard Grimes, the black minister of the Fugitive Slave Church, must have squinted into the sun just as I was doing as he emerged from his home at the rear of number 59 and turned left on his way to his church. Walking up Joy Street in December added new meaning to descriptions I had read about the sound of children sledding down its slope during the particularly snowy winter of 1850. And twisting my ankle on irregular cobblestone streets made clear the precarious footing for fugitive slaves fleeing at full run from slave catchers empowered by the Fugitive Slave Law of 1850.

Any historical event is much better understood within the context of its historical setting. It is one thing to read the details of the Battle of Gettysburg. It is quite another to stand on Little Round Top, with its commanding view of the battlefield to the north and west, and contemplate the assault of the 15th Alabama Confederates against the downhill charge of the 20th Maine Volunteer Infantry. Standing at the summit, taking the measure of the degree of slope and the open area that afforded little cover to advancing armies is an unforgettable experience. It also bears irrefutable testimony to the horror of that battle, the bloodiest of the Civil War, and to the sacrifice of the more than 50,000 men during four days in the summer of 1863.

The Landmarks of American History series has emerged from this belief in the power of place to move us and to teach us. It was with this same philosophy in mind that in 1966 Congress authorized the establishment of the National Register of Historic Places, "the Nation's official list of cultural resources worthy of preservation." These enduring symbols of the American experience are as diverse as the immigration station on Angel Island in San Francisco Bay, which served as U.S. entry point for thousands of Asian immigrants; or Sinclair Lewis's Boyhood Home in Sauk Centre, Minnesota, the place that inspired the novelist's Nobel Prize—winning descriptions of small-town America; or the Cape Canaveral Air Force Station in Florida, launch site of Neil Armstrong's historic trip to the moon. Taken together, such places define us as a nation.

The historic sites presented in this series are selected from the National Register, and they are more than interesting places. The books in this series are written by some of our finest historians—based at universities, historic museums, and historic sites—all nationally recognized experts on the central themes of their respective volumes. For them, historic sites are not just places to visit on a field trip, but primary sources that inform their scholarship. Not simply illustrations of history, they bring the reality of our past to life, making it meaningful to our present and useful for our future.

# How to Use This Book

T his book is designed to tell the story of American history from a unique perspective: the places where it was made. Each chapter profiles a historic site listed on the National Register of Historic Places, and each site is used as the centerpiece for discussion of a particular aspect of history— for example, Independence Hall for the Declaration of Independence, or the Woolworth store in the Downtown Greensboro Historic District for Martin Luther King Jr.'s role in the civil rights movement. This book is not intended as an architectural history; it is an American history.

On page 6 (opposite the table of contents), there is a regional map of the United States locating each of the main sites covered in this volume. Each chapter in this volume contains a main essay that explains the site's historical importance; a fact box (explained below); and one or two maps that locate the site in the region or show its main features. Each chapter also contains a box listing sites related to the main subject. For each related site, the box includes the official name, address, phone, website, whether it is a National Historic Landmark (NHL) or part of the National Parks Service (NPS), and a short description. As much as possible, the author has selected related sites that are geographically diverse and open to the public.

Many of the chapters feature primary sources related to the thematic discussion. These include, for example, letters, journal entries, legal documents, and newspaper articles. Each primary source is introduced by an explanatory note or a caption, indicated by the symbol ⚑.

At the back of the book is a timeline of important events mentioned in the text, along with a few other major events that help give a chronological context for the book's theme. A list of further reading includes site-specific reading, along with general reading pertinent to the book.

## Fact Boxes

Each chapter has a fact box containing reference information for its main site. This box includes a picture of the site; the site's official name on the National Register;

contact information; National Register Information System number (which you can you use to obtain more details about the site from the National Register, whose contact information appears at the back of this book); whether the site is a National Historic Landmark (NHL) or part of the National Park Service (NPS); and important dates, people, and events in the site's history.

Acts of Congress recognize and protect America's 386 National Park Service units, including National Parks, National Historic Sites, National Historic Battlefields, and National Monuments. The Secretary of the Interior designates National Historic Landmarks, of which there are more than 2,300. States, federal agencies, and Indian tribes have nominated the majority of the 75,000 properties listed in the National Register of Historic Places, some of which are also historic units of the National Park Service and National Historic Landmarks.

*Picture of site* ————

*Official site name* ————

## Valley Forge National Historic Park

*Contact information* ———— Valley Forge, PA 19482
610-783-1077
*Website* ———— *www.nps.gov/vafo*

*National Register Information System number* ———— NRIS 66000657
*Site is a National Historic Landmark/* ———— NHL, NPS
*National Park Service owns or maintains site*

*Date built or other significant dates* ———

**DATE OF ENCAMPMENT**
Winter 1777–78

*Architect, builder, or original owner* ———

**ORIGINAL OWNER**
Laetitia Penn, daughter of Pennsylvania's founder, William Penn

**SIGNIFICANCE**
*Summary of site's significance* ———
At Valley Forge Washington's army struggled to keep warm, overcame a poorly organized supply system, and summoned up the discipline and courage to renew fighting when spring arrived. The winter encampment became a test of the army's ability to survive, and therefore a test of the nation's as well.

# Preface

In considering which historic sites to include in this volume, I have relied on three touchstones in the study of history: place, time, and change. Place frames an event by providing a concrete setting for people's lives and providing a scale—whether it is a modest building in a village or grand city structure—for understanding how lives and events unfold. The time period when a person lives or when events occur also sets some of the parameters for understanding the possibilities and limitations of those lives and human experiences. For example, the options for women to participate in government and to enter the professional world are in part determined by the time period in which they live. And finally much of historical study revolves around the attempt to understand such changes as those of economy, education, and family life.

Change may occur at a snail's pace and be hardly noticeable, but at other times change is accelerated, with the periods immediately before and after being so markedly different that we refer to these periods as turning points. Moving chronologically from the experiences of Native American women in the fifteenth century to the historic preservation movement in the twentieth century, I have selected places to examine the broad themes of women's history. In specific places, it is possible to see the interplay between women's private and public lives as they have sought the right to vote, to participate in reform organizations, or to enter professions that had previously been reserved for males only. In some places, such as St. John's Freehold in Maryland's Historic St. Mary's City and Watervliet Shaker Historic District in Albany, New York, the dynamic personalities of Margaret Brent and Mother Ann Lee enabled these extraordinary women to claim religious and political roles usually denied to women of that time.

The buildings and archaeological sites in this book bring together these concepts of place, time, and change to explore some of women's experiences throughout American history. For example, the boarding house at

Boott Cotton Mill in Lowell, Massachusetts, illustrates the initial movement of women into the paid workforce in the 1820s, while the grand Gothic-style library built at Bryn Mawr College in 1907 reflects a growing trend of providing women with quality educational opportunities.

Some of the buildings in this volume I became familiar with when I coordinated the Women's History Landmark Project from 1989 to 1993. This was a cooperative effort of several national historical organizations and the National Park Service. The purpose of the project was to increase public awareness and appreciation of women's history by identifying significant sites and preparing nomination forms for their consideration for National Historic Landmark status. Some of the properties seem like old friends to me, for I assisted in shepherding them through the lengthy process of landmark designation.

Working on this volume has reminded me, however, that many properties important in the telling of the story of women's past have not been identified and placed on the National Register of Historic Places or have been destroyed. Since women often worked in informal ways and in modest conditions, there are frequently no buildings to document certain experiences. Suffrage newspapers, for example, were an important means by which the advocates of women's right to vote sought supporters. Yet women often worked on these newspapers out of rented space in unassuming buildings, and there is no evidence that any of these buildings are still standing.

For many years the bias in the historic preservation movement favored grand buildings associated with important men. However, new directions have evolved from the scholarship of the last three decades that has focused on the lives of ordinary people and groups who were often omitted from history books. The National Park Service has been taking the lead in encouraging the identification, preservation, and interpretation of historic places associated with women. Many of the buildings presented in this volume exist today as the direct result of Park Service policy to be more inclusive in its presentation of the past. The Park Service has accomplished this through the reinterpretation of existing National Parks, the establishment of new National Historic Parks, and the promotion of programs to increase the numbers of properties associated with women on the National Register and the National Historic Landmark program.

# Taos Pueblo

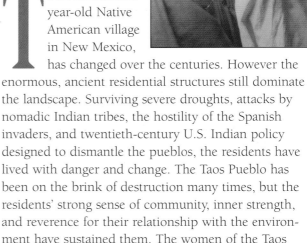

## Taos, N. Mex.

### Native American Women Building Community

The 1905 photograph titled "Taos Woman" (above) is one of 2,226 images in Edward Curtis's twenty-volume collection The North American Indian. A woman with a basket of bread at her feet and three children of the Taos Pueblo gather about a horno, a freestanding outdoor oven, in this 1902 photograph (below).

T he Taos Pueblo, a seven-hundred-year-old Native American village in New Mexico, has changed over the centuries. However the enormous, ancient residential structures still dominate the landscape. Surviving severe droughts, attacks by nomadic Indian tribes, the hostility of the Spanish invaders, and twentieth-century U.S. Indian policy designed to dismantle the pueblos, the residents have lived with danger and change. The Taos Pueblo has been on the brink of destruction many times, but the residents' strong sense of community, inner strength, and reverence for their relationship with the environment have sustained them. The women of the Taos Pueblo have been a major force in sustaining the community, for they were expert plasterers and the primary builders of homes, as well as the heads of their households.

The history of American women began more than 20,000 years ago with the migration of peoples from Asia by way of a narrow span of land that then linked Asia and what is today Alaska. Over centuries these peoples adapted to various regions of the country and created diverse cultures. Some led nomadic lives relying on hunting and gathering, and others settled in villages and grew their food. In the south-western part of the United States, the Native Americans made the transition from

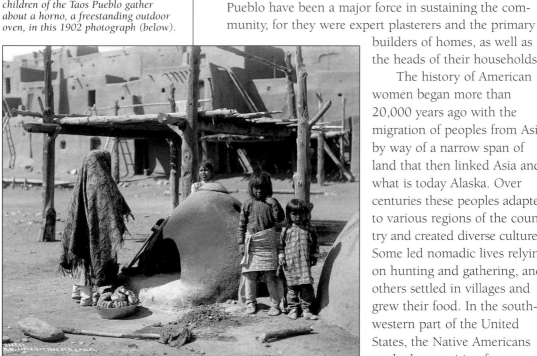

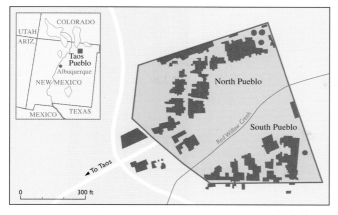

hunting to farming about two thousand years ago. The
growth and flowering of the Pueblo culture, which focused
on community life in individual settlements, occurred
around 1300. When the Spaniards arrived in 1540 there
were over a hundred widely scattered Native American
settlements in what is today New Mexico and Arizona,
many along the Rio Grande River. Each community had its
own government, religious practices, its unique pottery
and jewelry, and in many cases its own language. The
Spaniards gave these native Americans the name "Pueblo,"
which means village.

The residents of Taos Pueblo were an individual tribe
that was part of the southeast Native American village
culture, which is broadly defined as Puebloan. Since the
Taos tribe had no written language prior to the arrival of
Europeans, knowledge of their early history comes from
pictorial records, songs and legends taught by tribal
elders to each generation, and from recent archaeological and scientific studies of early tools, land, and buildings. The tribe understands its origins to be associated
with Blue Lake, located in the mountains high above the
pueblo. It is to Blue Lake that the Taos Indians have
gone for centuries for some of their most sacred and
secret ceremonies. Legend is that the Taos Pueblo was
founded by a great chief who followed an eagle and led
his people to a sparkling stream at the foot of the mountains. When the eagle dropped two plumes, one on each
side of the stream, the chief took this as a sign that this
was where they were to build their permanent homes.
Red Willow Creek, which provides the drinking water
for the Taos Pueblo, has its source in Blue Lake.

The first historical description of the Taos Pueblo
comes in 1540 from Hernando Alvarado, one of the

*This early twentieth-century Taos ladder, measuring over seven feet high, is made of two side posts with five wooden cross pieces latched together with leather and slender supporting splints. The principal means of entering the adobe houses and underground kivas, ladders have become a symbol of Taos Pueblo life.*

members of Francisco Vasquez de Coronado's expedition of several hundred Spanish soldiers. Alvarado described the Taos Pueblo as comprising two large buildings, one on each side of the river, each covering about two acres and each about five or six stories high, with each story becoming narrower as they rose to the top. Although these structures are often characterized as two buildings, they are actually two clusters of multilevel buildings with narrow passageways between them. The massive, ancient buildings appear to have been built haphazardly as family living units made up of several rooms and built on top of each other. Each story was set back a number of feet from the rooms below. A wooden corridor extended around the circumference of each story, creating a terrace and serving as a walkway. People entered each apartment from the roof by a ladder through a hatchway. There were no doors and few windows visible on the exterior of the buildings and the openings in the roofs that served as entranceways were the major sources of light.

On the high walls at the corner of the structure were fortified towers. Since the residents did not enter the houses on the ground floor but instead had roof hatchways, the villagers, if attacked, could remove the ladders and climb to the top terraces, where they could aim their bows and arrows at the invaders. Women assisted in the defense, mainly by communicating with loud cries or smoke signals to nearby allied communities.

These large apartment buildings had hundreds of rooms, and each family had several chambers. Though the structures had a few wooden beams to support the walls and roof, they were essentially made of adobe, a sun-dried mixture of straw and mud that was covered with a protective yellowish-brown plaster made of lime and clay. The Taos Indians had little furniture, but the rooms had poles for hanging clothes and small niches in the thick walls that served as cupboards. They used the rooms for sleeping, storing food and clothing, and for protection from the bad weather. Most of the daily activity took place on the roof terraces and in the plaza areas. A wall, probably as much as eight feet high when it was originally built, surrounded the two large structures and the plaza area. Serving as added protection for the village, the wall had openings for shooting at the enemy.

The Taos Pueblo has seven kivas, large underground ceremonial chambers central to the spiritual life of

Pueblo tribes. Four kivas are located inside the historic walled city and three just outside the wall. Openings in the ground with ladders sticking up marked the location of these sacred gathering places. The kivas are distinguishable from the dwelling spaces in that they are larger and are generally circular. Reflecting the awe with which the historic Pueblo tribes regarded women's fertility, the kivas were considered the womb of Mother Earth. These underground womb-caverns were where spiritual birth took place and where the residents of the Taos Pueblo became renewed and transformed.

Life at Taos Pueblo centered on the community rather than the individual, and the focus of attention was on providing food, clothing, and shelter and caring for and protecting the next generation. The typical household was composed of a woman and her husband, married daughters and their families, and unmarried sons. All of the family members looked up to the elder woman of the household for instruction and advice.

Women in Pueblo society were highly respected. In addition to building the homes, their duties included meal preparation, making pottery and textiles, and caring for the children. They also had authority over the family's few possessions. The men had responsibility for cultivating the nearby fields, governing and defending the village, and presiding over religious ceremonies. In this scheme of daily life neither women nor men were subordinate to the other, and their separate responsibilities were equally valued. This pattern of mutual service represented to the Taos residents the balance and harmony of nature. Women, with their ability to reproduce, were seen as reflecting the earth. Men, who cultivated the fields, were identified with the sky and with the sun and rain that made crops grow. Thus the union of the female and male qualities produced the children and the crops on which the tribe relied.

Women, with limited assistance from men, built the houses in the Pueblo villages. The men placed the cedar logs for the roof, with the ends protruding through the walls. Onto these beams the women placed mats of branches on which they lay grasses, then covered the new roof with a thick layer of mud and a finishing coat of adobe plaster. Although adobe often refers to construction made from sun-dried bricks, the Pueblo women in the period before the Spanish did not make

## Taos Pueblo

Taos, NM 87571
505-758-1028
*www.taospueblo.com*
NRIS No. 66000496
NHL

**DATE BUILT**
1325

**ORIGINAL AND CURRENT OWNER**
Taos Indian Pueblo

**SIGNIFICANCE**
The Taos Pueblo is one of the best preserved of the early Pueblo villages. Residents have inhabited its oldest structures for more than 700 years. Although the village has experienced much change over the centuries, it still retains some of the original features from the time the women of the village, who were the major builders, constructed the two enormous clusters of buildings.

*Fragments of Taos ceramic pottery dating from approximately 1200 have been pieced together to reconstruct this bowl, which has a black and white geometric border. From ancient times to the present, Pueblo women have excelled in creating objects that are both beautiful and useful.*

bricks. Instead they used a process known as puddling, which resulted in very thick walls. The women would form with their hands a thick layer of mud and straw and when it had dried they added another layer on top. Layer upon layer they built the wall to the needed height and then applied a mixture of plaster over the puddling layers, using a sheepskin to give the wall a smooth and protective finish. Each year women gave the houses fresh coats of mud plaster to protect them from the heavy summer rains. Made out of the earth, the houses frequently crumbled in some spots, and women had the never-ending job of preparing new plaster to make repairs.

The extraordinary role that women played in house building surprised many of the early Spanish visitors. The priests of the early missions at Taos found it inappropriate for women to build houses and tried unsuccessfully to get men to take over this task. One of the priests wrote: "If we compel any man to work on building a house, the women laugh at him. . . and he runs away."

Much of women's time was spent in preparing food for a diet that consisted primarily of corn, beans, and squash. Women fixed corn, the central food, in a variety of ways—boiled, roasted over a fire, or ground into a fine powder that could be used to make bread. Each day women ground corn. Using a large hollowed-out stone, women moved a pestle back and forth with both hands to grind the corn into meal. Food preparation was often a community undertaking with one woman crushing it, another doing the initial grinding, and a third grinding it finer. One of the tribe's distinctive foods was pika, a thin bread made with blue cornmeal and baked quickly on a hot stone slab.

The dress of Pueblo women, called a manta, was a black one-piece tunic that covered only the right shoulder and often had colored embroidery. It was gathered at the waist by a woven belt. They wore sturdy moccasins to protect their feet from the cacti and thorns of the region. Pueblo women wore all types of jewelry—necklaces, bracelets, and earrings—made of turquoise, shell, bone, seeds, stone, clay beads, and coral acquired through trade with Pacific Coast tribes. In the nineteenth century, after increased contact and trading with the Spanish and the Mexicans, Pueblo women began to wear brightly colored clothes.

Ceremonies, often related to the seasons, held a prominent place in the Pueblo society. While some of their ceremonies were held in the mountains above the village at Blue Lake, the most sacred shrine of the Taos Indians, many were held in the kivas or in the plaza inside the walls of the pueblo. With the drum as the basic musical instrument, the Pueblo people engaged in songs and dances that depicted the planting, cultivating, and harvesting of corn. There were rituals and prayers for rain and other conditions favorable to the crops, as well as for thanksgiving for a bountiful harvest or a successful hunt. The ancient Taos racetrack, which ran for a half-mile along the river, figured prominently in some of the ceremonies. There were races for the Sun and Moon to give these celestial bodies power to travel and to regulate their courses.

Weddings were very special events at the Taos Pueblo. The courtship process that led to marriage had a very set pattern. On the occasion of rabbit hunts, young women gave corn cakes to the young men in exchange for a rabbit. If a young woman gave a specific young

*A post fence surrounds the entrance to this kiva, one of five underground chambers at the Taos Pueblo where the community has assembled for centuries for tribal gatherings, sacred dances, and ceremonies. A ladder with poles extending high into the sky provides access to the subterranean room where no visitors are allowed.*

# The Roles of Native American Women

The roles and responsibilities of Native American women throughout the area that would become the United States varied according to tribal traditions and customs and were in part determined by the opportunities and demands of the different regions.

The Iroquois, who lived in the Northeast, depended on women not only to care for the home but to do the farming. The women even joined men on fishing expeditions. In matters of tribal governance, when a local chief died, it was a clan of elder women who nominated a successor. Some early visitors to Iroquois villages considered the women to be slaves of the men. However, to the contrary, the consensus among modern anthropologists and historians is that the women maintained the tribe and held significant authority.

Among the Cherokees of the South East and Middle West, women maintained the home and also had sole responsibility for farming. Women produced cooking pots and vessels for water, wove cloth for blankets and garments, and made baskets and tools for use in their agricultural work. Cherokee women were especially well known for their deerskin moccasins. They sewed these moccasins with needles they constructed of bone and thread made of deer sinew. In Cherokee tribes the family organization centered around the wife's lineage, with women owning the houses and the fields.

The women of the tribes who lived on the Great Plains—which included the Cheyenne, Blackfoot, Sioux, and Pawnee—were the architects and builders of tipis, the tribes' dwellings. Since these tribes migrated often in their hunt for buffalo, it was necessary to have lightweight but sturdy and easily constructed housing. The tipis were cone-shaped tents with three or four main interior poles tied together to provide a frame and then covered with buffalo skins. Women, often working in groups, prepared the buffalo hides, then designed and made the tipis. Flaps allowed for ventilation, making it possible to build fires in the larger tipis. These flaps could also be used to close the tipis tightly against winter storms and heavy rains. When the tribes migrated to new encampments, it was the women who selected the location for the tipis.

*A Ute woman constructs the frame for a teepee in 1913. When the Plains Indians moved their camps, horses dragged these long poles piled with their belongings.*

man all of her corn cakes, this was a signal that she would welcome his attention. If he then visited her, the relationship became official. She would then take blue corn cakes to his house. If he ate them all, this was an indication that he wished her to become his bride. He then began, with help from his father and uncles, to weave wedding robes. The prospective bride, with assistance from her mother and aunts, began grinding a large supply of corn flour that she then delivered in baskets to the home of her prospective husband.

Just before the wedding, the bride's mother washed the groom's hair with yucca seeds and the groom's mother did the same for the bride. The groom's father scattered sacred cornmeal on a path from his house to that of the bride. The ceremony began with the bride and groom clothing each other with special blankets made for the occasion. Then they received gifts, which played a key part in the wedding ceremony. The bride received gifts of earthenware and a grinding stone to signify her cooking responsibilities, and the groom received a bow, spear, and war club to signify that he was to protect his wife and children. During the ceremony a hoe was placed in his hand to signify that he was to grow the food. Then the bride and groom each carried a handful of cornmeal and walked to the edge of the village. They breathed on the cornmeal and threw it to the sun. When they returned from the walk, they were husband and wife. The bride received two blankets from her husband. The large one she wore at the wedding and the smaller one she saved to be draped over her at her death.

Of the over one hundred pueblos that the Spaniards found when they first explored the area that is now New Mexico and Arizona, fewer than one-fourth remain today. While there have been considerable changes over the past five centuries, one of the best preserved is the Taos Pueblo. The eight-foot protective adobe wall that surrounded the village has diminished to four feet due to natural deterioration and lack of maintenance. Yet one can still see the loopholes through which the Taos tribe could shoot at the enemy.

As a result of the Spanish occupation of the pueblo and the arrival of the first priest at Taos in 1598, the mission church of San Geronimo occupied a prominent place inside the walled village. Many of the Taos Pueblo's current residents have houses with modern conveniences close to or actually in town. Although the historic church was destroyed in 1847, the ruins are still visible. The church that stands today inside the walled pueblo was built in 1850 and is called the San Geronimo Chapel. For many years the high houses of the Taos Pueblo sheltered the entire tribe, but in the last several centuries numerous individual adobe residences, as well as shops and roads, have been constructed inside the walled village. Yet efforts have been made to maintain the pueblo's historic appearance, including the placing of electric lines underground. The Pueblo's casino, located a few miles from the historic village, provides significant income for the Pueblo.

The large multi-storied family dwellings are the most distinguished feature of the Taos Pueblo, and they retain much of their original appearance, although doors have been added on the ground level and there are more windows today than when the pueblo was first built. However, the simplicity and mystique of the massive walls still present a striking image as the structures narrow with each elevation, the units arranged on top of each other in irregular fashion. These two clusters of buildings, the largest adobe structures in the United States, blend dramatically into the desert and mountains that surround them.

Taos Pueblo is among the most photographed and painted sites in America. Ansel Adams, one of America's foremost photographers, has made these ancient buildings the subject of many of his photographs. The United Nations Educational Scientific Cultural Organization (UNESCO) has placed the Taos Pueblo onto its World Heritage List, along with such noted places as the Egyptian Pyramids and the Vatican City in Rome

The ever-expanding tourism industry contributes needed income, but also endangers the historic landscape of the Taos Pueblo. Yet the Taos Pueblo in the twenty-first century retains many of its traditional practices and remains a vital Native American community. Women with their traditional skills of making baskets, pottery, and textiles make needed money today to help in supporting their families, and this preservation of tribal crafts has fostered a sense of tribal identity and pride.

*To enter the Balcony House cliff dwelling in Mesa Verde National Park, visitors must climb a thirty-two-foot ladder, crawl through a twelve-foot-long tunnel, and then climb an additional sixty feet on ladders and stone steps.*

## CHACO CULTURE NATIONAL HISTORICAL PARK

Nageezi, NM 87037
505-786-7014
*www.nps.gov/chcu*
NPS

Between 850 and 1250 AD Chaco Canyon was a major center in the development of Puebloan culture, serving as a hub of ceremony, trade, and tribal coordination. With skillful planning and construction, the Chacoan people created an urban center of spectacular public architecture. Thirteen major ruins, as well as hundreds of smaller ones, may be seen there today. Among the ruins is a great house, called Pueblo Bonito, which had over 600 rooms and was four stories high. It is one of the most extensively excavated and studied sites in North America and a place sacred to many American Indian groups.

## MESA VERDE NATIONAL PARK

Near Cortez and Mancos
Mesa Verde, CO 81330
970-529-4465
*www.nps.gov/meve*
NPS

Mesa Verde, located in the southwest corner of what is now Colorado, was for more than 700 years the home of the ancestors of the Pueblo tribes. From approximately 600 through 1300 AD people lived and flourished in communities throughout the area. During the last century of this period, the residents of Mesa Verde, which in Spanish means "green table," built villages of cliff dwellings in the sheltered alcoves of the canyon walls. In the late 1200s a severe drought, lasting more than two decades, forced them to abandon their villages and move out of the area. The archaeological sites at Mesa Verde are some of the most notable and best preserved in the United States. They provide insights into the relationships between the early development of Puebloan culture and their contemporary descendants who still live in the Southwest today.

## KNIFE RIVER INDIAN VILLAGES NATIONAL HISTORIC SITE

Stanton, ND 58571
701-745-3309
*www.nps.gov/knri*
NPS

Along the Knife River, researchers have identified more than forty archaeological sites that provide clues about the lives of the Plains Indians who probably lived here as early as 5000 BC. Archaeological findings document the transition in village life from relying primarily on hunting, supplemented by gathering of wild foods, to depending on agricultural labor supplemented by hunting. Large circles of raised earth with sunken centers, from thirty to sixty feet in diameter, are all that remain of the numerous earth lodges inhabited by the Hidatsa and Mandan Plains tribes.

The archeological remains of the earth lodges reflect the peak of the Hidatsa and Mandan culture during the eighteenth century. The land, which was cultivated by the women, and the earth lodges, also built by the women, were passed down from generation to generation by the female line. The women were responsible for growing and preparing food, maintaining the lodges, making pottery, and caring for children. The men focused on making weapons, hunting, fishing, seeking spiritual knowledge, trading, and protecting the village.

# St. John's Freehold, Historic St. Mary's City

## St. Mary's City, Md.

### Settling the New World

*Margaret Brent (above), romanticized in this charcoal drawing, ignored customs and assumed a public role as a successful landholder, business woman, and public figure. Information about her life can be gleaned from a few surviving historical records and from the archeological excavations (below) at St. Mary's City.*

Trying to reconstruct the lives of colonial women is a difficult task. For the period before 1700, there are very few surviving diaries and letters by women. The large majority of women lived in rural areas in one- or two-room houses that vanished from the landscape long ago. Yet documents such as wills with household inventories, ship logs, and the records of courts, governing bodies, and churches as well as other findings of archaeological research, provide some clues to understanding the lives of the first European immigrants to North America.

One of colonial America's remarkable women, and one whose history has survived in a few intriguing documents, is Margaret Brent. On January 21, 1648, Brent went before the governing assembly of the colony of Maryland to request a right to vote. This unusual and dramatic event took place in St. John's Freehold, a home that doubled as the meeting place for the colony's governing body. Brent, a single woman, was a prominent landowner, a business agent, and the administrator for the estate of the governor of Maryland, Leonard Calvert, who had recently died. Since women in this period were barred from participating in the political arena, this was a daring request. Although the Assembly denied Brent a vote, she executed the will of the deceased governor in an able and courageous manner, winning the admiration of the leaders of the young colony during a time of unrest and revolt.

Margaret Brent was an intelligent and adventuresome woman who had left Gloucestershire, England, at the age of thirty-seven with her sister Mary and two brothers, Giles and Fulke. They arrived in Maryland on November 22, 1638, just five years after the founding of the colony. Their family had not only wealth, but also connections. Margaret's father was a Lord, as was her mother's father. Among the Brents' distinguished distant relatives was Cecil Calvert, also known as Lord Baltimore, who in 1632 had secured the charter to establish the Province of Maryland from King Charles I. Like the Calverts, the Brents were seeking new economic opportunities. But equally important, both families were Roman Catholics, and at that time in England, Catholicism was officially condemned. The Brents and the Calverts wanted a place where they could freely practice their faith.

When Margaret and her sister Mary landed at St. Mary's City, they had in their possession an important letter. Dated August 2, 1638, the letter was from Lord Baltimore to Governor Leonard Calvert, and gave instructions that Margaret and Mary Brent should have a grant of "as much Land in and about the Town of St. Maries and elsewhere in that Province in as ample manner and with as large privileges as any of the first adventurors have." Since the size of the initial land grants in St. Mary's was based on the number of servants the colonists brought with them, the fact that Margaret and Mary had with them four maidservants and four men gave them a privileged status. Margaret quickly presented her letter to Governor Leonard Calvert and on October 4, 1639, obtained from the Maryland Assembly a grant for seventy and one-half acres in St. Mary's City. Subsequently, she and her sister added fifty adjoining acres and a thousand acres on Kent Island to their holdings.

Margaret and Mary called the house they built "Sister's Freehold." The term "freehold" was frequently used in St. Mary's to signify land that was not leased or

## St. John's Freehold, Historic St. Mary's City

St. Mary's City, MD 20686
800-762-1634
*www.stmaryscity.org*
NRIS No. 69000310

**DATE BUILT**
1638

**ORIGINAL OWNER**
Provincial Secretary John Lewger

**SIGNIFICANCE**
As the meeting place for the provincial council of the Maryland colony as well as the home of Provincial Secretary John Lewger, St. John's Freehold was the building where Margaret Brent, the first woman landholder in Maryland and the executor of the estate of the colonial governor, appeared before the provincial assembly in 1648 to seek the right to vote.

loaned but was fully owned and free of any obligations. The Sister's Freehold was a tobacco plantation about a ten-minute walk from the center of St. Mary's City. Little is known about the house, which disappeared from the landscape a few hundred years ago; but archaeologists have been able to determine its approximate location on the St. Mary's River, one of the many rivers of the Chesapeake Bay area.

In addition to raising the cash crop of tobacco for an international market, Margaret Brent was a business agent on whom a number of planters relied. To work their fields, these planters depended on indentured servants, men and women who worked without wages for a period of time in exchange for transportation to the American colonies. Brent served as a broker for importing and placing indentured servants, and often arranged loans for new settlers. She furnished supplies such as sugar and spices to planters. Additionally, county records show that a number of settlers on different occasions asked her to handle legal matters and bestowed on her the power of attorney. Her skills as a manager were well recognized. Her brother Giles and Governor Leonard Calvert both engaged her to oversee their land. With all of her business ventures, she frequently appeared in the court to collect debts and address other aspects of her business dealings.

Some people today refer to Margaret Brent as the first woman lawyer in America. It was the practice in the seventeenth century for well-educated property owners to conduct their own affairs in court, but it is well documented that Margaret made appearances in court acting on behalf of other planters in St. Mary's. Since many early colonial courts had no professional standards for becoming a lawyer, there was no licensing process. Yet today, in recognition of her legal skills, the American Bar Association gives an annual Margaret Brent Award to an outstanding woman lawyer.

Two factors enabled Brent to handle legal affairs: she had been well educated in England and she was a single woman. Under the English common law that was practiced in America during this period, a married woman was legally bound to her husband and had no independent legal standing. However, single women over the age of twenty-one had legal rights to make contracts and hold property in their own names.

Margaret Brent's leadership role evolved in the 1640s, a time when local conflicts in Maryland mirrored the hostilities in England, where Protestants and Catholics were waging civil war. In Maryland, a Protestant named Richard Ingle led a rebellion against the Calverts, who were Catholics. Leonard Calvert succeeded in putting down the rebellion, but died of an undetermined cause before he was able to pay off the soldiers he had recruited to assist him. On his death bed, when he put Brent in charge of settling his estate, he told her to "Take all, pay all." In order to prevent mutiny, Brent had to pay the soldiers. Realizing that Leonard Calvert's estate was not large enough to cover such expenses, she had to raise the necessary funds and went before the Provincial Court on January 3, 1648, to request that Leonard Calvert's power of attorney for his brother Cecil Calvert, also known as Lord Baltimore, be granted to her. This authority allowed her to collect rents and in emergency situations to sell property belonging to Lord Baltimore. The assembly granted her this request.

When Brent appeared before the assembly a few weeks later, she asked for one vote for herself, since she was a landowner and all landowners were entitled to a

*The first extensive excavation of St. John's Freehold to use principles of scientific archaeology began in 1972. This early work, which included recovering the foundation and nearby deposits of trash and pottery, stimulated interest in uncovering the lost history of the seventeenth-century settlements of the Chesapeake Bay.*

vote, and another vote as Lord Baltimore's legal representative. Thomas Greene, who became governor after Leonard Calvert's death, considered her request but refused her the right to vote. The assembly's records for January 21, 1648, state:

> Came Mrs Margaret Brent and requested to have vote in the howse for herselfe and voyce allso for that att the last Court 3d Jan: it was ordered that the said Mrs. Brent was to be lookd uppon and received as his [Lordship's] attorney. The Govr denyed that the [said] Mrs Brent should have any vote in the howse And the sd Mrs Brent protested agst all the proceedings in this [present] Assembly unlesse shee may have vote as [aforesaid].

Although no one knows what Brent's motives were in going before the assembly to request the vote, she clearly had significant administrative responsibilities that required ongoing interaction with the assembly. In her role as executor of the estate of Lord Baltimore, she may have wanted the vote to seek the appropriation of tax money to pay the soldiers. Whatever the basis of her request, she was the first woman in America to appear before a governmental body and ask for the right to vote, and she did this two hundred and fifty years before women in the United States finally gained that right.

Immediately after the assembly refused her request for the vote, Brent began to sell some of Lord Baltimore's cattle to pay the soldiers. When Lord Baltimore learned of this and expressed his displeasure, the Maryland Assembly wrote to him and not only defended but praised Margaret Brent's action: the soldiers were hungry and angry at not being paid as they had been promised; she had acted swiftly to avert a crisis. The assembly told Lord Baltimore that his estate was better off in Margaret Brent's hands than in those of any man's, for the soldiers had treated her

*Cecil Calvert, also known as the second Lord Baltimore, secured the charter in 1632 from King Charles I to establish the first privately owned English colony in the New World. As the rulers of the colony, the Calverts, who were Catholic, adopted a policy of religious tolerance, allowing Christians of many types to worship as they wished.*

with respect. The assembly also acknowledged that her abilities had contributed to the "publick safety" and played a major role in preserving the stability of the colony. Yet by this action she lost favor with Lord Baltimore, and in 1651 she moved to Virginia, where she lived until her death in 1671.

The building where Margaret Brent made her plea for the right to vote was a home called St. John's Freehold, located a short walk around the pond and past the town mill from the center of St. Mary's City. One of the most important structures in town, it was built in typical English style in 1638 by John Lewger, the first secretary of Maryland. He named it, as was the custom among Catholics at the time, for his patron saint and included the designation of "freehold" to emphasize his ownership, clear and free, of the property.

St. John's Freehold was the center of operation for Lewger's 1,000-acre tobacco plantation. But also, prior to the building of a State House in 1676, St. John's Freehold served as the meeting place for the provincial assembly and the court. Over the years various additions were made to St. John's Freehold, but it was originally a one-and-a-half-story frame building, twenty feet wide

*The Historic St. Mary's City Commission constructed wooden frames to outline the structure of the lost buildings above some archeological foundations. The use of what they refer to as "ghost frames" helps visitors visualize this seventeenth-century town, whose remains are mostly below ground.*

# Maryland Indentured Servant Writes to Her Father

 *Elizabeth Sprigs, a young woman who came to the colony of Maryland as an indentured servant, wrote a pleading letter on September 22, 1756, to her father, John Sprigs, who lived in London. In the letter she asked for forgiveness for leaving her family, describing her desperate condition, and requests that he send her clothing and shoes. This letter is one of the few existing accounts of what life was like for a female indentured servant.*

Honred Father
Maryland Sept'r 22'd 1756

My being for ever banished from your sight, will I hope pardon the Boldness I now take of troubling you with these, my long silence has been purely owning to my undutifullness to you, and well knowing I had offended in the highest Degree, put a tie to my tongue and pen, for fear I should be extinct from your good Graces and add a further Trouble to you, but too well knowing your care and tenderness for me so long as I retaind my Duty to you, induced me once again to endeavour if possible, to kindle up that flame again. O Dear Father, believe what I am going to relate the words of truth and sincerity, and Ballance my former bad Conduct [to] my sufferings here, and then I am sure you'll pitty your Destress[ed] Daughter, What we unfortunat English People suffer here is beyond the probibility of you in England to Conceive, let it suffice that I one of the unhappy Number, am toiling almost Day and Night, and very often in the Horses druggery, with only this comfort that you Bitch you do not halfe enough, and then tied up and whipp'd to the Degree that you'd not serve an Annimal, scarce any thing but Indian Corn and Salt to eat and that even begrudged nay many Negroes are better used, almost naked no shoes nor stockings to wear, and the comfort after slaving dureing Masters pleasure, what rest we can get is to rap ourselves up in a Blanket and ly upon the Ground, this is the deplorable Condition your poor Betty endures, and now I beg is you have any Bowels of Compassion left show it by sending me some Relief, C[l]othing is the principal thing wanting, which if you should condiscend to, may easely send them to me by any of the ships bound to Baltimore Town Patapsco River Maryland, and give me leave to conclude in Duty to you and Uncles and Aunts, and Respect to all Friends

> Honred Father
> Your undutifull and Disobedient Child
> Elizabeth Sprigs
>
> Please to direct for me
> at Mr. Rich'd Crosses to
> be left at Mr. Luxes Merc't
> In Baltimore Town Patapsco River
> Maryland.

and fifty-two feet long, with two major rooms and an attic with additional sleeping and storage areas. There was a large chimney in the center of the house with a bedroom on one side and the parlor on the other. The large bedroom was also Lewger's office and was where he kept tax and property records and processed wills. The parlor served as a meeting place for the provincial court, assembly, and council. All that remains today of St. John's Freehold is the archaeological excavation of its stone foundation, cellar, and chimney.

Margaret Brent, who made an unprecedented plea for the right to vote at the Assembly meeting at St. John's Freehold, was not typical of the women who lived in St. Mary's City in the 1630s and 40s. Most women during the town's first decades were indentured servants. In exchange for paid transportation to the colonies, these women committed themselves to a period of labor, often four or five years. Unlike the New England colonies in the seventeenth century, where most immigrants came as families and for religious reasons, most of the women immigrants to Maryland came as individual indentured servants. Most of them were Protestants and did not share the Calverts' commitment to a colony for Catholics. They were adventuresome types seeking to improve their economic standing; many had been attracted by advertisements that promised rewarding opportunities in the new world.

*These five thimbles are among the artifacts uncovered by archeologists at the Historic St. Mary's City Commission. Thimbles were useful and treasured items for colonial women, who, among many other tasks, sewed new garments and repaired old ones.*

In St. Mary's City there were six men for every woman, and as a result, female indentured servants in St. Mary's City could expect to marry. Their hope was that following their four-or-so years of servitude, they would become planters' wives. Many of the pamphlets published in England for use in recruiting indentured servants claimed there would be no heavy fieldwork, but this did not always turn out to be the case. Growing tobacco is labor intensive; and some planters had a shortage of workers and expected their male as well as their female indentured servants to do hard agricultural labor. By the early eighteenth century, when the southern colonies began to develop and expand, planters with extensive land used slaves from Africa, and not indentured servants of European descent, to work the fields.

The promotional material that sought to attract women indentured servants to St. Mary's also implied that a prospective husband could pay for the remainder of a woman indentured servant's time and that she could escape much of her obligation of servitude. It is not known how often this happened, however. Recent research does reveal that women indentured servants in St. Mary's City had no fathers or family members to press unwanted suitors on them, so at least they had freedom in choosing a mate. This was not the custom in New England, where fathers dictated many of the decisions of their daughters.

Whether a woman was an indentured servant or a planter's wife, she worked hard. Only a very few planters had household servants. Keeping the fire going, baking bread, growing vegetables, pounding corn, churning butter, preparing meals, milking cows, brewing cider, keeping chickens, sewing clothes and quilts, washing clothes, and caring for children—these were her tasks. Wives often performed all of this work while pregnant or nursing babies. Additionally, the new immigrants faced the risk of becoming ill with malaria or flu.

Death was an ever present factor in St. Mary's City, as in other European settlements in America. Many women died in childbirth, for on the average they were pregnant every two years. In St. Mary's City an estimated 25 percent of children died during their first year.

In a startling statistic, historians Lois Green Carr and Lorena Walsh, in their study of planters' wives in seventeenth-century Maryland, found that after seven years of marriage, it was likely that one partner had died and that after ten years, only one third of marriages were still intact. Since many in St. Mary's remarried soon after a spouse's death, there were complex family structures. Many children had half-sisters and half-brothers, as well as stepmothers and stepfathers. Children in the Chesapeake colonies referred to their father's wives as "now-wives" as a way of dealing with the complexities of remarriage.

In the mid-eighteenth century, a hundred years after Margaret Brent, woman profited from some of the changes in colonial society. They were able to purchase some of the goods they had previously had to make, and life for most was not as harsh as it had been for the earliest settlers. Interestingly, the number of women who remained single increased during the colonial period. This may well have been due to the fact that only single women had legal control over their property. It would be over a century before some aspects of women's inferior legal status changed and almost two centuries before women gained the vote.

While some colonial women in the eighteenth century were shopkeepers and engaged in various types of entrepreneurial work, the vast majority of women in all the colonies up and down the east coast were farm wives, giving birth to many children and responsible for endless chores.

From 1633 to 1695, when the capital moved to Annapolis, St. Mary's City grew from the original settlement to a bustling village of approximately two hundred year-round residents. The seventeenth century was the golden age for St. Mary's. After it ceased to serve as Maryland's capitol, it all but disappeared. The many crude wooden houses and the few grander wooden structures, as well as a handful of brick buildings, burned or fell down and scavengers carried off what reusable materials they could find. The once thriving village returned to open fields with no aboveground structures from the seventeenth century

*In 1992 archaeologists excavated three lead coffins at the site of the Brick Church. Scientists discovered much about the people whose remains were found in the two larger coffins, including what time of year they died and what type of food they ate.*

remaining. Yet the rural setting on the banks of the lovely St. Mary's River remained the same.

Today historic St. Mary's City is a well-preserved colonial archaeological site with an outdoor museum that uses historical records combined with the evidence of archaeology to piece together life in Maryland's first capital. Replicas of the Maryland Dove, the ship that brought the first settlers to Maryland in 1634, the State House built in 1676, and several other buildings help to evoke the atmosphere of this colonial town. Historic St. Mary's City has placed simple building frames, called ghost frames, above the grounds of the old city to mark the location where seventeenth-century buildings once stood.

Many of the homes were typical of those in other colonies in that they consisted of one large room. A large fireplace dominated the wall and served as the kitchen area. Along another wall were one or more beds, and in the center of the room were a table and chairs. Sometimes a ladder reached to a loft where there were additional beds. Privacy as we know it today did not exist in colonial households.

Archaeologists, who systematically study evidence from past cultures, consider St. Mary's to be one of the few totally "vanished" cities in America. It is a particularly important archaeological site in that it is the only remaining seventeenth-century town in America that has remained relatively undisturbed, with no new buildings ever constructed at its location. Pioneering excavations began at St. Mary's City in the mid-1930s, following the grand 300th anniversary celebration of the founding of Maryland. In 1966 the state of Maryland established the Historic St. Mary's City Commission, which has the mission of rediscovering this old city and the lives of those who lived in it. St. Mary's City holds particular fascination for historians of women's history because it was the home of Margaret Brent.

## BRICK CHAPEL

St. Mary's City, MD 20686
240-895-4990
*www.stmaryscity.org*
NHL

The first church in the new colony of Maryland was a wooden chapel that was built in 1639 and burned down a few years later. In 1667 the Jesuits, a Catholic order that had been a major investor in Lord Baltimore's colony, replaced it with a fine brick chapel that was constructed in the shape of a cross. The dimensions of the center portion were fifty-four feet long and twenty-four feet wide. There were arched windows along each side and a high rounded ceiling. The extensions on either side had a total measurement of fifty-seven feet. The floor was made of imported stone and the roof of tile.

Archaeologists began excavations of the ruins of the Brick Chapel in 1990, and in 1992 they discovered three lead coffins, a sign of great wealth. Careful research revealed that two of the coffins held the remains of Philip Calvert, a former Governor and high-ranking official in Maryland, and his wife Anne Wolseley Calvert. Sharon Long, a renowned specialist in constructing human likeness from skulls and other available evidence, created through an elaborate process a facial sculpture of what Anne Wolseley Calvert may have looked like.

## WILLIAM SMITH'S ORDINARY

St. Mary's City, MD 20686
240-895-4990
*www.stmaryscity.org*
NHL

William Smith's Ordinary, which was a combination hotel, restaurant, and bar, was the center of social, economic, and political activities in St. Mary's City. The ordinary (which refers to an ordinary table where anyone, regardless of status, could be served a meal if able to pay) was located among a cluster of buildings in the heart of the town, along with offices, a printing house, shops, and a church. Women were the principle workers in the ordinary, preparing and serving food and drink. Built in 1666, the ordinary measured twenty feet by thirty feet and was constructed by placing posts deep into the ground. It completely burned to the ground just twelve years after it had been constructed. Smith's Ordinary is one of the few buildings in Historic St. Mary's City that have been reconstructed. Based on extensive findings from the archaeological excavations, the replica of the ordinary helps to capture the seventeenth-century life at St. Mary's City.

*The Historic St. Mary's City Commission has reconstructed this ordinary, where visitors can have a lunch of seventeenth-century food such as pottage (soup) and seafood stew.*

# Watervliet Shaker Historic District

## Albany, N.Y.

### Leading Religious Communities

*Watervliet's South Family, about 1870, enjoys some leisure time outdoors. Behind them are the family buildings, which surround an open common area, an arrangement similar to college quadrangles.*

Throughout American history from the eighteenth century until the twenty-first, women have not only made up the majority in religious congregations but they have also provided leadership. While many denominations have restricted women's behavior, American society has had a climate receptive to experimentation. Some very exceptional women have responded to God's call and established new ways of worship and ministry.

One of the earliest and most influential women religious leaders was Mother Ann Lee. In 1774, just two years before the Revolutionary War started, she founded the first permanent settlement of the religious group officially named the United Society of Believers in Christ's Second Coming, but generally known as Shakers. The Shakers sought to create a perfect society in which everyone worked diligently, worshiped God, shared all their possessions, denounced marriage, and lived an orderly and simple life. A foundation of the Shakers' belief was an understanding of God based on the existence of an Eternal Father and an Eternal Mother. As Father, God is the almighty, the powerful, the most holy; and as Mother, God is love and full of tenderness.

Mother Ann was a multifaceted person who presents a challenge to those who wish to understand her. She was illiterate but was intelligent, with a keen mind. She required of her followers an extremely orderly life yet she embraced a style of worship that included spontaneous dancing with leaping

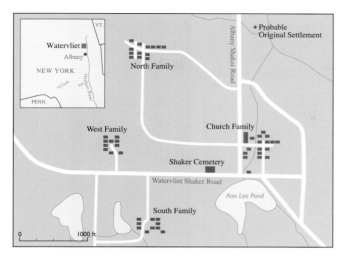

The Shaker Community at Watervliet, seven miles northwest of Albany, New York, formed four large family groupings, each self-sustaining with its own cluster of buildings. The families derived their names from their locations in relationship to the Church Family, where the community had its main meetinghouse. Mother Ann Lee is buried near the oldest family unit, the Church Family.

and bowing. Her early followers in their reminiscences described her as being of common stature for a woman, thickset but straight, well-proportioned, and regular in form and features. Her complexion was light and fair, and she had blue eyes and light-chestnut brown hair. Yet her most distinguishing feature was the penetrating glance that inspired confidence and respect. While she strongly felt the deep corruption and wickedness of human beings, she was a cheerful person. She was very efficient and practical but she also had heavenly visions and divine revelations.

The journey of Ann Lee, from a poor family in England to founder of a religious group in America, was filled with hardship and determination. Born in 1736 in Manchester, England, Ann Lee started work in a textile mill in England when she was only eight years old. As a child she had no opportunity to go to school, and never during her life did she learn to read or write. She developed an astounding memory, however, and in her later years could recite much of the Bible. When her mother died, Ann became responsible for her young brothers and sisters. In 1758 when she was twenty-two years old she heard the electrifying preacher George Whitefield.

The Whitefield religious revival proved to be a turning point in Ann's life. Although she had been raised in the Church of England, which in its American form became the Episcopal Church, she became an active participant in the "Shaking Quakers," a small group inspired by a French sect. The group's name described the way the worshipers' spiritual excitement led them to shout, shake, and dance. The Shaking Quakers held the

*The Shaker commitment to separate spaces for men and women and to order can be seen in their dancing lines. All the men on the right side of the room face the women on the left.*

unusual belief that Christ would come to earth again soon in the form of a woman. Jane Wardley, one of the leaders of the Manchester Shaking Quaker community, frequently proclaimed that God was both male and female and that Jesus had represented the male side of God and the female side was yet to be revealed.

At the age of twenty-six, under pressure from her father, Ann married Abraham Stanley, a blacksmith. Revealing her strong independent streak, Ann Lee never used her husband's name. They had four children, and each was a difficult birth. Three died as babies and the fourth at the age of six. Following the death of her young daughter in 1766, Ann experienced debilitating grief and guilt. Although half of the children of Manchester's working-class parents died before the age of five, Ann took on herself the responsibility for her children's deaths and convinced herself that sex and marriage were the root of evil.

Several years later Ann became one of the leaders of Manchester's Shaking Quakers and was arrested for leading noisy meetings and disturbing the order of the town. While in prison she had a vision that revealed to her that evil in the world was rooted in sexual lust. She then proclaimed that the way to gain spiritual strength was through celibacy and the self-denial of all sexual relations. She vowed she would never again have sexual relations with her husband. In a surprising turn of events—and an indication of Ann's persuasive powers—her husband, who at first was furious at her, decided to join the Shaking Quakers.

In the face of increasing hostility toward the Shaking Quakers, Ann was again imprisoned. This time while in solitary confinement she experienced a visitation from Jesus, and said he had told her that she was to be his anointed successor on earth. She told her followers that "It is not I that speak, it is Christ who dwells in me." Her followers interpreted her mystical revelations as evidence that she was the human incarnation of Christ's femininity and the spiritual Mother for whom they had been awaiting.

From this point, Ann Lee's followers called her Mother Ann. Her teachings stressed a shared communal life, celibacy, the dignity of work, an adherence to order and efficiency, and worship that was simple and joyful. She spoke frequently of the dangers in a religion that had clergy, creeds, and a rigid form of worship. Since Mother Ann left no writings, most of what is known about her comes from accounts by her followers. "Testimony of the Life, Character, Revelations and Doctrines of Our Ever Blessed Mother Ann Lee, and the Elders with Her" was published in 1816 in Hancock, Massachusetts, over thirty years after her death. It provides, from her followers' perspective, detailed information about her life and teachings.

The persecution of the Shaking Quakers and George Whitefield's return to Manchester, when he told of his evangelical tours in America, helped to convince Mother Ann that she should lead a mission to the New World. The initial enthusiasm for emigration among many members of the Manchester Shaking Quakers soon faded, but even so, John Hocknell, one of the few wealthy persons attracted to the Shaking Quakers, sponsored the voyage. Hocknell and his son and Ann's brother William were among the eight followers who sailed in 1774 to New York, where they worked at various jobs to support themselves while they searched for a place to settle.

They decided on a tract of land of dense forest near Albany, New York, and Mother Ann started her first colony in an area known by the Native Americans as Niskayuna, called Watervliet by the descendants of the Dutch settlers of the region, and now known as the town of Colonie. In 1775 the Shakers began construction of

## Watervliet Shaker Historic District

875 Watervliet-Shaker Road
Albany, NY 12211
518-456-7890
*www.cr.nps.gov/nr/travel/pwwmh/ ny16.htm*
*www.crisny.org/not-for-profit/ shakerwv*
NRIS No. 73001160

**DATE BUILT**
Settled in 1776, surviving buildings date from 1820

**ORIGINAL OWNER**
United Society of Believers in Christ's Second Coming, generally known as Shakers

**SIGNIFICANCE**
Established by Mother Ann Lee, Watervliet was the first permanent Shaker settlement. Its style of worship and community life, including a disciplined and communal daily routine and a distinctive approach to worship that included dancing and leaping, served as the pattern for other Shaker settlements.

their first building, a log cabin. Establishing a self-sufficient community located on swampy land at what was then the edge of civilization proved difficult, especially during the unusually harsh winters. During the first few years, the Shakers constructed a few crude log buildings, drained the swamp to make farmland, created the Mill Pond, and grew enough food to avoid starvation. Like the Puritans of their time, the Shakers worked hard and preached simplicity.

Unlike the Puritans, the Shakers delighted in expressing their exalted feelings in jubilant and spirited songs and dances. They believed that the gift of song held a distinguished place in their lives, uniting feelings of joy with thanksgiving for God. Joyful praise, the Shakers felt, was the appropriate response after having confessed their sins, received forgiveness from God and had Him dispel for them the gloom and sorrow of this world. Their teachings stated that God turned "mourning into dancing." Building on the musical traditions of the Hebrews, Shakers placed singing and dancing at the core of their worship. They looked forward to what they called the "everlasting Jubilee," when the rich and the poor, the high and the low, the bonded and the free, male and female, all would become one in Christ Jesus, creating a perfect community with love as the bond of their union. One of the early Shaker hymns that came

*Elder Josiah Barker and seven sisters of Watervliet's North Family in 1912. To preserve their modest image, all the women wore long, simple dresses.*

from the Watervliet community was entitled "Come to Zion," and it proclaimed the glories of the jubilee, a time of rejoicing.

Despite their determination and zeal, no new members joined during the first four years of the Shaker community at Watervliet. Mother Ann recognized that the Shaker way was not for everyone but still sought—unsuccessfully in those first years—to inspire new believers to join the community. She made a symbolic connection between the temple as a place of worship and our bodies as "living buildings." The words of a Shaker hymn emphasize the relationship of spiritual and physical bodies: "Leap and shout, ye living building; Christ is in his glory come; Cast your eyes on Mother's children; See what glory fills the room."

The first hardbound Shaker hymnal, *Millennial Praises*, published in 1813 in Hancock, Massachusetts, included a lengthy hymn, titled "Mother," that tells of the early years at Watervliet. The eleventh verse of this sixteen-verse hymn states:

> Near Albany they settled
> And waited for a while,
> Until a mighty shaking
> Made all the desert smile.
> At length a gentle whisper,
> The tidings did convey
> And many flocked to Mother
> To learn the living Way.

While many of their hymns dealt with themes of praise, love, and work, some retold the pivotal episodes in the growth of the Shaker communities. The religious revivals in the area in the 1780s created a receptive climate for the Shaker mission, and finally their numbers began to grow. In 1781 Mother Ann and five of her followers embarked on a spiritual crusade in New York and Massachusetts, preaching rejection of worldliness and proclaiming the joys of communal life in over thirty-six towns. Singing joyfully all the while, they taught everyone they met the Shaker songs of greetings, gifts, and farewell. One of their most successful stops was at Mount Lebanon, New York, located about twenty-six miles from Albany, where a number of people became ardent followers of Mother Ann.

The hardship of the extended trip, which lasted three years, combined with the outright hostility they

*By hanging their chairs upside down from hooks on the wall, the Shakers were able to sweep the floors easily and to maintain their high standards of cleanliness. Superb craftsmen, the Shakers built furniture that was useful and graceful, with no unnecessary ornamentation.*

*Male worshippers enter the Mount Lebanon Meeting House using the door on the left, and the women use the door on the right. This Second Meeting House, as it was called, was built in 1824, after the community had outgrown the first. The building has a barrel roof and a strong foundation to support the dancing that was basic to Shaker worship.*

experienced on several occasions, took its toll on Mother Ann. She never fully regained her strength and died in 1784. Yet Mother Ann's followers carried on her work.

The Mount Lebanon Shaker Society, founded soon after Mother Ann's death, became the headquarters for the movement and directed the affairs of the other communities. It was at Mount Lebanon in 1788 that the Shaker Society was officially organized. Mount Lebanon leaders, whom Mother Ann Lee won over to the Shaker faith during her visit, subsequently wrote the Millennial Laws, the principles of belief that guided all the Shaker communities in their faith, conduct, and communal administration. These laws also set forth directions on how Shaker communities were to construct their buildings, thus accounting for the similarity of the buildings among the Shaker communities. In 1800 there were eleven Shaker communities in the United States and by 1820 there were twenty-four.

Following the principles for communal life adopted at Mount Lebanon, the Watervliet community built its first family structure, the South Family dwelling, in 1800. As membership increased, the Watervliet Shakers established additional "families," the Church, North, West, and South Families, whose names were determined by their location in the community in relation to the main meetinghouse. Although not a traditional family, the Shakers believed that a spiritual relationship was stronger than blood ties. They lived as brothers and sisters in separate but equal spaces. A planned community evolved at Watervliet, replacing the original rustic log cabins that had existed in Mother Ann Lee's lifetime. The Watervliet Shakers never had more than 350 members at one time. The early part of the nineteenth century marked their high point. By 1839 they had a thriving religious community, prosperous businesses, and owned 2,500 acres of land.

The family houses, or dwelling houses as they were often called, usually had a basement, three main floors, and an attic. And this was the case at Watervliet. The large dining room and the kitchen, with other rooms for baking and canning vegetables and jams, were in the basement. A distinguishing interior feature of the dining room was the row of pegs on the wall, where chairs were hung at the conclusion of each meal, a custom that facilitated the sweeping of the floors and illustrates the importance that Shakers placed on cleanliness.

The meeting rooms and the bedrooms, or "retiring rooms" as they were called, were on the main floor. The dwelling houses each had one wing for brothers and another for sisters, located on opposite ends of the house and divided by a spacious hall. Two to six people lived in a room. There were double doorways, double stairways, and double retiring rooms so that men and women would each have their separate spaces. In the family houses only two rooms were shared by men and woman, the dining room and the meeting room, but even when sharing these spaces, men and women sat at opposite ends of the room. Family members gathered several times a week for worship in the meeting room. They also had smaller gatherings in their private rooms where four to ten brothers or sisters would spend an hour in conversation and song.

There were children in the Shaker communities. However, no children were ever taken into the community except at the request of their parents. The Shaker approach to child rearing was one of great care and gentleness. The Shaker

*"In the Emblem of the Heavenly Sphere" portrays the Shaker artist's vision of heaven. The four people on the top row are (from left to right) Mother Ann Lee; her brother William; James Whittaker, who was a faithful follower; and Christopher Columbus, who was probably included because he discovered the New World, the chosen home of the Shakers. Because Shakers did not believe in decorative items, they considered these "gift drawings" holy relics, not pictures to be hung on the wall.*

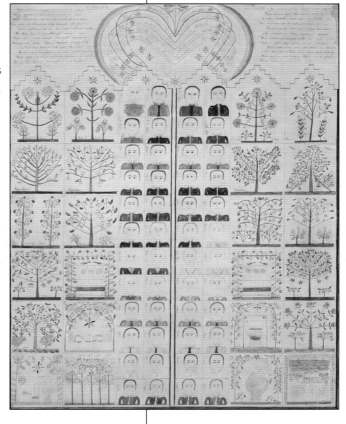

schools had a reputation for emphasizing religious instruction, having fine libraries, excelling in instruction, and providing a pleasing environment for the children.

Each family house had its own individual gardens, fields, and workshops, with at least one brothers' shop and one sisters' shop for each family where goods were produced for sale. Generally speaking, the women took care of the household duties and the men did the heavier agricultural chores, but under pressing conditions everyone pitched in to do whatever was needed.

Shunning anything elaborate, the Shakers constructed their residences, workshops and places of worship with utmost attention to creating efficient buildings with stark, clean-cut lines. Principles of functionality and simplicity informed the Shaker way of life and guided their architectural designs. While the buildings at Watervliet resembled simple farm buildings of the period, there was evidence of the Shaker spirit in the uniformity of the rectangular buildings with their low-pitched roofs, symmetrically spaced windows, and center doorways.

Shakers were master builders who constructed buildings that were strong and orderly with reliance on right angles and prescribed spaces for specific activities with separate areas for men and women. There were no blueprints. The builders and carpenters adapted the building's form to its function and followed their basic tenets of sturdiness and simplicity. As their model they used traditional rural building types and not what they referred to as "fanciful" designs, and they incorporated a concern for economy and ease of maintenance. Shaker buildings tended to be well proportioned, without any ornamentation that was not functional, and often had a simple hood or canopy over the entrance. Each community used the materials that were most plentiful in their areas.

A rigorous daily schedule was at the heart of Shaker life. Each family dwelling house had a bell on the roof to signal the rising hour and meal times. In their everyday lives, Shakers functioned as disciplined "living buildings," cutting their bread and meat in squares and never diagonally, walking on right-angle paths, and holding themselves upright. Those who slouched or nodded had to make a public apology.

Shakers supported themselves by growing their own food, making their own clothes, tools, and equipment,

*This colorful package of string bean seeds is one of the products that the Watervliet Shakers sold to earn money to sustain their community. In keeping with their spirit of practical innovations, the Shakers were the first to develop a commercial operation for gathering and packaging small quantities of seeds for family gardens.*

and producing items to sell to support the family. At Watervliet the two major products were packaged seeds and brooms. The Watervliet Shakers were the first people in the country to sell garden seeds as a commercial product. The garden seeds business became quite profitable beginning around 1811, and by 1840 the community was earning thousands of dollars annually from the sale of seeds. Other Shaker communities specialized in clocks, baskets, textiles, or furniture.

Today the Watervliet Shaker Historic District includes twenty-two buildings that comprise some of the best examples of Shaker architecture in existence. All of these buildings were constructed after Mother Lee's death. In the 1920s a fire destroyed all of the buildings of the North Family, and over time many of the workshops and agricultural buildings of the other three families have either fallen down from neglect or been torn down. However, three of the family domestic structures have survived, as well as meeting houses, workshops, wash houses, barns, and other agricultural structures such as a dairy, granary, and wagon shed. The West Family dwelling house, which has been converted into apartments, is one of the best preserved with the least exterior modification of all Shaker buildings that are still standing in the United States.

Although some of the remaining buildings have had significant modifications since the nineteenth century, the rural setting and the placement of the structures, with the buildings of each family organized at right angles, has been retained. The open spaces between the families has been maintained and still creates an impressive visual impact. Since 1977 the Shaker Heritage Society operates an outdoor museum that features a self-guided walking tour of the Church Family, which still has eight of its early-nineteenth-century structures. Additionally, there is a large area of archeological significance with evidence of the blacksmith shop, carriage house, machine shops, and a dining house.

During and after her life in the eighteenth century, Mother Ann has stirred controversy. Her critics have stressed her preoccupation with "lust" and her claim of a divine commission from Christ. Yet she is also remembered as the founder of one of America's most successful experiments in creating a utopian religious community in which members strive for perfection in their daily lives, own no possessions, and share their communal resources. The music of the Shakers has lived on in the compositions of the noted composer Aaron Copland, whose well-known symphony, "Appalachian Spring," builds on the melody of the Shaker hymn "Simple Gifts." The renowned American dancer Martha Graham, who helped to develop modern dance, elaborated on Shaker dances. The principles of functionality and simplicity in Shaker architecture remain a viable part of the American tradition. Shaker furniture, with its attention to excellence in craftsmanship, is prized by contemporary museums for its simple grace and beauty. The Shakers' adherence to order, the lack of clutter in their lives, and the way they balanced spirituality and practicality in their daily life have resonated with many modern Americans. There is no doubt that despite the fact that the Shaker religion has died out, Mother Ann has left a powerful legacy.

The religious rivals of the eighteenth and nineteenth centuries created a climate that encouraged Christians to focus on their individual spiritual experiences more than on the rules of the church. This emphasis on personal experience opened the way for various forms of female religious leadership. Since most established denominations objected to ordaining women as ministers, a few exceptional women followed Mother Ann Lee's path of founding new denominations: Ellen White was a co-founder in 1863 of the Seventh Day Adventist Church; Mary Baker Eddy founded the Church of Christ, Scientist in 1875; and Aimee Semple McPherson established in 1921 the International Church of the Foursquare Gospel.

## ELMSHAVEN

125 Glass Mountain Lane
St. Helena, CA 94574
707-963-9039
707-963-0861
*www.elmshaven.org*
NHL

Elmshaven, built in 1885, was Ellen White's home in her later years, from 1900 to 1915. The home and its setting reflect White's commitment to the concerns for which she advocated throughout her life: vegetarianism, clean air, the virtues of country living, water therapy, and a commitment to education. Set on a small hill, the house is surrounded by orchards, vegetable gardens, and a spring with therapeutic waters. Nearby is a rural health retreat.

## ANGELUS TEMPLE

1100 Glendale Boulevard
Los Angeles, CA 90026
213-273-7000
*www.dreamcenter.org*
NHL

Built in 1921, Angelus Temple is an exceptional building with a large dome that rises 125 feet. Beneath the dome is the main auditorium, which has two balconies and seats more than 5,000 people. Wearing a distinctive white dress and blue cape, Aimee McPherson preached at Angelus Temple every night and three times on Sunday, stressing the need for spiritual repentance and personal reform.

## MOUNT LEBANON SHAKER SOCIETY

U.S. Route 20
New Lebanon, NY 12125
518-794-9500
*www.shakerworkshop.com/ mt_leb.htm*
NHL

The Mount Lebanon Shaker Society was the largest and most influential of Shaker communities and served as the administrative center in the United States for the Shaker movement. Established in 1787, three years after the death of Mother Ann, Mount Lebanon Shaker Society had, at its peak in the nineteenth century, 600 members in a village of 100 buildings on 6,000 acres. In 1929, with only a few surviving members, the community sold the land and buildings to the Darrow School. Thirty-five of the original Shaker buildings are still standing.

## MARY BAKER EDDY HOUSE

12 Broad Street
Lynn, MA 01902
781-593-5634
*www.cr.nps.gov/nr/travel/ pwwmh/ma53.htm*
*www.marybakereddy.org*

Mary Baker Eddy lived in this house from 1875 to 1882. It was in the front parlor of this house where she first held services and where she formally established the Church of Christ, Scientist. This house is now a museum, owned and run by the Christian Science Church.

*The parlor where Mary Baker Eddy first held her Christian Science classes is equipped for religious gatherings with a pump organ and a number of chairs. This Lynn, Massachusetts, house is now a museum furnished with some of Eddy's own pieces as well as other items of the period.*

# Boardinghouse at Boott Cotton Mill, Lowell National Historical Park

## Lowell, Mass.

### Working in the Mills

*American artist Winslow Homer made this woodcut (above) of a young girl standing before a loom threading a bobbin. The power looms used in the Lowell Mills had bobbins that fit into shuttles that moved back and forth across the loom, carrying the yarn that was woven into cloth.*

The Boardinghouse at Boott Cotton Mill at Lowell National Historical Park is a place that illustrates well how in the 1830s significant numbers of American women were entering into the world of paid employment. Most women had worked prior to this time, but their work was primarily as slaves, indentured servants, or in their homes and on the family farm. Although their contributions were substantial in agricultural production, caring for chickens, food preparation, sewing shoes, and making cloth, candles, and soap, most women did not work for money. From the colonial period, there had been some women who earned income from work such as traders, merchants, teachers, or midwives, but these entrepreneurial women were the minority.

In the decades between 1790 and 1830 the United States experienced major technological advances during what is often called the industrial revolution, a time when new machines, tools, and sources of power fostered momentous changes in manufacturing. Before the Civil War, Lowell, Massachusetts, was the largest center of textile production in the country, with ten large mills turning out a total of 50,000 miles of cotton cloth a year.

During the initial stage of the industrial revolution in America, numerous small mills appeared on the rivers of New England, using water power to run machines for spinning yarn. The further development of steam-powered looms to weave cloth led to the building of larger mills in urban areas. In the early nineteenth century the completion of a canal to connect Lowell to the major port in Boston laid the foundation for the rapid expansion of Lowell as a textile center. Wealthy Boston merchants began construction of the Lowell mills in 1822. Kirk Boott, one of the Boston entrepreneurs and

an engineer, oversaw the project, designing the buildings and laying out the streets.

Massive five-story factory buildings lined the canals.
Great, thick, red brick walls surrounded the interior
courtyard spaces of mills that could be entered only by
crossing a single bridge over the deep water of a canal.
Dominating the central courtyard of the Boott Mill was
the bell tower, whose chimes controlled the lives of the
workers. The bells awakened employees, called them to
meals, signaled the beginning and end of the work day,
and announced the ten o'clock curfew, when all boardinghouse residents were to be in their rooms.

The investors in the new textile industry in Lowell
had a great supply of raw cotton from the South, water-
wheels and turbines to produce power, machines to
accomplish the various stages of making cloth, and an
economical means of transporting their goods to Boston.
But they needed a reliable workforce. Concerned that
England's factory towns had become associated with
unsafe, filthy, and immoral conditions, the Lowell textile
owners set about creating a mill village that would
attract the young single girls who worked on farms in
the region and whose reliability and competence had
already been established. Another reason the mill owners were attracted to the idea of hiring young women
was because they could pay them a lower salary than
they would have to pay men. In addition, they assumed
that young women would probably marry and drop out
of the workforce after a few years. The owners considered this likelihood an advantage because it meant that

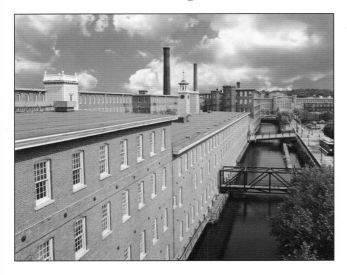

*The Boott Canal ran between the
Merrimack River and the Boott Mills.
It was part of six miles of canals that
powered ten major mills, which at
their peak employed more than 10,000
workers. The water channeled out of
the river into canals and fell into the
buckets of a waterwheel to produce the
energy that drove the looms.*

*A large group of young women gathers outside a Boott Mills boardinghouse in 1870. By 1900 mill owners had subdivided the boardinghouses into tenement apartments for the immigrant families who had replaced the New England farm girls as the majority of laborers in the textile mills.*

*Lowell Mill owners used elaborate labels to identify bolts of cloth. The label heading gave the Mill's name and manufacturing location, while the center featured colorful images of the production of cloth, and the bottom gave the incorporation date and provided a blank space for the identification number of the bolt.*

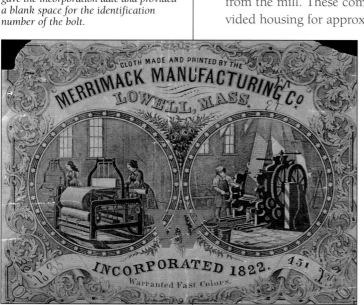

women were less likely to develop into a working class that would strike and rebel against working conditions. The Lowell mills had a revolving workforce. For every young woman who left after a few years to return home to marry, two others would arrive seeking work.

The first communal living units built by the textile companies in Lowell were two-and-a-half-story wooden structures. In the mid-1830s, the design shifted to larger three-and-a-half-story brick rowhouses, which could accommodate more residents. In the 1830s the Boott Cotton Mills built eight rows of boardinghouses across from the mill. These company-built boardinghouses provided housing for approximately 75 percent of the female textile workers. Although these boardinghouses were destroyed some years ago, the Lowell Historic Preservation Commission reconstructed one of the boardinghouses in the 1980s and it is now part of the Lowell National Historical Park.

Each of the Boott Cotton Mill's eight long residential buildings contained four boardinghouse units, similar to dormitories, located in the center of the building. On each end was a tenement section that included apartments with individual kitchens. The single women lived in the boardinghouse portion of the rowhouses and skilled male workers who had families lived in the tenement sections. The rowhouses for workers were large, measuring 150 feet long and 36 feet wide. Built in the early Georgian style of architecture known for simplicity, uniformity of detail, and symmetry, the boardinghouses had regularly spaced tall chimneys, gabled-roof dormers, and symmetrically placed windows. Each of the boardinghouse units had a communal dining room and parlor. These rooms as well as the kitchen and the supervisor's room were on the first floor. The upper floors were for bedrooms, and there were often about ten bedrooms to a boardinghouse. Four to eight women usually slept in a bedroom with two women sharing each of the double beds, making for cramped living conditions.

Young women made up 85 percent of the workforce in the mills in Lowell in the 1830s and more than 80 percent of these women were between the ages of fifteen and thirty. Thousands of young women from the farms of New England migrated to Lowell to work in its ten largest textile miles. Agents employed by the mills traveled about the rural areas of New England promising young women good wages and decent living conditions. For farm families, having a daughter work in the mills meant one less mouth to feed at home as well as an additional source of income for the family. Wages also offered the opportunity to buy a special dress, shoes, or piece of jewelry as well as to save some money for a dowry, the property and funds that a bride brought to her marriage.

As the owners had expected, most young women worked for less than six years in the mills and then married. However, they usually did not work for several continuous years but instead worked for repeated short stretches with frequent visits back home to help with the family farm. Sometimes in the summer factories closed down when the water in the rivers was low due to dry spells.

The workday in the mills was long and hard. A mill bell rang at 4:30 AM to awaken the employees and an hour later the iron gates of the mill closed. Late employees had to enter by a special entrance where they often had their wages reduced and received a scolding. The mills were noisy, the air filled with cotton dust, and the tasks tedious and repetitive. To keep the threads from

## Boardinghouse at Boott Cotton Mill, Lowell National Historical Park

Merrimack Street
Lowell, MA 01852
978-970-5000
*www.cr.nps.gov/hr/travel/pwwmh/ma48.htm*
*www.nps.gov/lowe*
NRIS No. 76001972
NHL NPS

**DATE BUILT**
1835–1838

**SIGNIFICANCE**
The Boardinghouse at Boott Cotton Mill at Lowell National Historical Park, which commemorates American women's entry on a large scale into the world of paid employment, provided communal living units for the unmarried female textile workers and gave the textile corporate managers considerable control over their lives.

*This 1848 engraving of the Merrimack Manufacturing Company boarding-houses shows the massive brick building with rows of dormer windows and chimneys along the roof line. In the foreground is a tree-lined street with fenced-in yards. The initial plan of the mill owners was to create pleasant living quarters for their workers.*

becoming dry and brittle, the work areas were kept humid and hot in the summer. The windows were always closed, so there was no ventilation to provide for fresh air or cool breezes. The poor air quality made the workers susceptible to various lung diseases. The daily schedule included a thirty-five minute break around noon for lunch, and the closing bell did not ring until six or seven o'clock. Almost all the jobs required the women to stand all day before machines whose many moving parts at times caused injuries, some just cuts and bruises but others quite serious, such as the loss of a hand. Millworkers generally worked Monday through Friday for twelve hours each day in the winters and even longer in the summer. On Saturdays they had a shorter day, only eight hours.

A woman's level of experience determined her work assignments. Beginners, called spare hands, served as assistants while learning the necessary skills and were at the bottom of the pay scale. Those engaged in carding and spinning were on the next lowest rung. Carders worked the machine that combed and straightened the fibers and then combined and twisted them into loose cords, called roving, that was wound gently onto tall wooden cylinders. The spinners monitored the machines with rows of spindles, each with a bobbin, that took the roving from the carder machine to make finished thread. Spinners had to quickly replace the filled bobbins with empty ones. The weavers who operated the looms that produced finished cloth were among the most experienced and highest-paid workers. Men held all of the supervisory positions.

In 1836, most of the Lowell mills paid spare hands about forty-four cents a day, spinners received fifty-eight cents a day, and weavers sixty-six cents a day. The male workers who repaired the machines made $1.27 a day and the overseer made $2.09 a day. Since the young women living in the boardinghouses had to pay about five dollars monthly for their room, meals, and laundry, this left them with about ten dollars a month. While some of the "mill girls" used a portion of this money to upgrade their farm clothing with more sophisticated urban fashions, most of the female employees managed to save twenty-five to fifty dollars a year. This was much more than a young woman would ever have earned on the farm and may well have been more cash than her father had. For many young women this money became a nest egg they hoped would allow them to start their own families, and for a few it provided a means to further their schooling.

The average worker in the Lowell mills was a young single woman who had left the family farm to come to Lowell. Frequently she came with a sister or cousin. The

## Sarah Bagley: Advocate for Labor Reform

Sarah Bagley began work in the Lowell textile mills in 1836, when she was eleven years old. In 1840 she wrote about her experiences in the *Lowell Offering* and described them in a very positive way. However, with declining wages and deteriorating working conditions, including the speeding up of machine operations, Bagley became critical of the mill owners. She founded the Lowell Female Labor Reform Association, which initiated a campaign that sent petitions with 2,000 signatures to the Massachusetts Legislature detailing the poor working conditions and calling for a law to limit the workday to ten hours.

In February 1845, when the special legislative committee held hearings, Bagley was among those testifying. The March 1845 Massachusetts House Document described the hearing and Bagley's testimony and reported Bagley as saying: "The chief evil, so far as health is concerned, is the shortness of time allowed for meals. The next evil is the length of time employed." The Massachusetts legislature in 1846 voted to reject the mill workers' petition. Little is known about Bagley's life after that except that she successfully secured a good job as the superintendent of Lowell's new telegraph office.

extended family network helped new workers acquire good positions and housing by alerting them to how the system worked and on occasion by having a relative put in a good word for them with the supervisor. But whether one had a relative there or not, the boardinghouses provided a community of support. Though the workers put in long hours in the factories, they also enjoyed their limited free time with young women their own age with whom they could go window-shopping or on outings in the countryside. A few would splurge on a holiday train trip to Boston. The female workers created their own standards of how to talk, dress, and behave—with a strong bent toward shedding unfashionable country clothes and replacing the rural dialect with a more polished manner of speaking.

The Lowell system of factory management included not only clean and well-run boardinghouses for its workers but also various self-improvement programs for after-work hours. In addition to the many religious and

*The replica of a bedroom in the reconstructed Boott Mill Boardinghouse is a pleasant but crowded room with a fireplace, mantle, and pictures on the wall.*

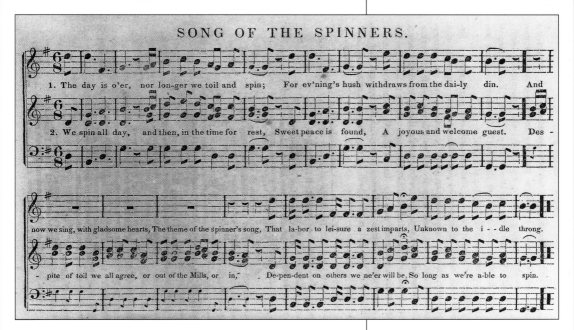

SONG OF THE SPINNERS.

1. The day is o'er, nor lon-ger we toil and spin; For ev'ning's hush withdraws from the dai-ly din. And

2. We spin all day, and then, in the time for rest, Sweet peace is found, A joyous and welcome guest. Des-

now we sing, with gladsome hearts, The theme of the spinner's song, That la-bor to lei-sure a zest imparts, Unknown to the i--dle throng.

-pite of toil we all agree, or out of the Mills, or in, De-pen-dent on others we ne'er will be, So long as we're a-ble to spin.

social activities sponsored by the nearby churches, there were lectures, plays, and programs at the libraries.

The best known of these cultural opportunities was the *Lowell Offering,* a magazine that evolved from an evening church group where the young women read their writing to each other. The mill owners provided the financial backing for the magazine, which was written and published by mill girls from 1840 to 1845. It included articles about nature, science, and religion as well as poetry and short stories. Those workers who wrote for the *Lowell Offering* did not generally question the policies or actions of the mill owners and accepted a secondary role for women. Harriet Farley, a textile worker who was also the editor of the *Lowell Offering* for three years, recognized the owners' support but denied that they controlled the magazine. Instead she viewed the *Lowell Offering* as providing young women with an opportunity to gain respect for their literary abilities. Several noted British authors, including Charles Dickens and Harriet Martineau, visited Lowell and were most impressed with the abilities of the young women who produced the *Lowell Offering.*

Despite the relatively peaceful nature of the Lowell workforce, the young women did engage in a protest in 1834 when the mill management announced a cut in wages. Approximately 800 women joined in a march to the center of the town where, the *Boston Transcript*

*This sheet music about the life of spinners appeared in an 1842 issue of the* Lowell Offering, *the literary magazine written by the Lowell mill girls. The song celebrates time for "sweet peace" following a day of toil in the noisy textile mills.*

# Escape through Creative Writing

*A longing for home and the unspoiled beauty of the rural landscape were frequent themes in the pages of the* Lowell Offering, *a newspaper written by and for the young women who worked in the mills. Elizabeth E. Turner, one of the New England farm girls who had come to work in the Lowell Mills, wrote this article titled "Factory Girl's Reverie," which appeared in the* Lowell Offering *in 1845. In the article Turner contemplates her life at the mill as well as others' perceptions of "factory girls."*

## FACTORY GIRL'S REVERIE

Tis evening. The glorious sun has sunk behind the western horizon. The golden rays, of sunset hues, are fast fading from the western sky. Gray twilight comes stealing over the landscape. One star after another sparkles in the firmament. The bird, that warbled its plaintive song through the long day, has pillowed its head beneath its wing. The prattle of playful children is hushed. The smith's hammer is no more heard upon the anvil. The rattle of noisy wheels has ceased. All nature is at rest.

Evening is the time for thought and reflection. All is lovely without, and why am I not happy? I cannot be, for a feeling of sadness comes stealing over me. I am far, far from that loved spot, where I spent the evenings of childhood's years. I am here, among strangers—a factory girl—yes, a factory girl; that name which is thought so degrading by many, though in truth I neither see nor feel its degradation.

But here I am. I toil day after day in the noisy mill. When the bell calls I must go: and must I always stay here, and spend my days within these pent-up walls, with this ceaseless din my only music?...

*The cover of the August 1845* Lowell Offering *shows a well-dressed, attractive young woman strolling along a canal with book in hand. A question on the cover about Biblical prophets and the church steeple in the background indicate the importance that the mill owners placed on regular church attendance, which they required of all boardinghouse residents.*

reported, one of them gave a "flaming…speech on the rights of women and the iniquities of the 'monied aristocracy.'" For several days, the young women refused to go to the mills. The mill owners, faced with rising competition, held firm on the reduction in pay and in a few days the workers returned to their jobs. A protest two years later, however, was successful. At that time the female mill workers organized a slow-down of production to protest an increase in rates at the boardinghouses. A third of the female workers in Lowell participated. After several months, the mill owners abandoned their plan to charge higher prices for room and board. In the 1840s women in Lowell joined in the broad labor movement sweeping across New England that demanded a reduction in hours and called for a ten-hour day.

The owners saw a connection between the solidarity that the workers gained from the boardinghouse culture and the labor protests. Thus by mid-century the owners had shifted their policies and no longer built boardinghouses but instead required newcomers to board with local families or live in tenements. The recruitment of young farm girls, that had been known as the "Lowell system," was abandoned around 1850 as the mill owners sought cheap immigrant labor. But the boardinghouses that had attracted the early farm girls produced female wage earners and a female culture that is an important chapter in American women's history.

The Lowell mills began a slow decline in the early twentieth century as the mills aged and modern, rival textile mills emerged in the South. It was not until the 1970s that Lowell's rebirth began as political and business leaders envisioned the revitalization of the downtown to preserve an important development of this nation's labor and industrial history. In 1978, as a result of a growing appreciation for industrial architecture and the need to preserve historic buildings of national significance, Congress established the Lowell National Historical Park. Visitors today can see the restored Boott Cotton Mills, which include extensive interpretive exhibits, the network of canals with their locks, St. Anne's Church where the young women were required to attend services, the corporate housing built in the 1840s for the mill agents, as well as the reconstructed boardinghouse for the "mill girls."

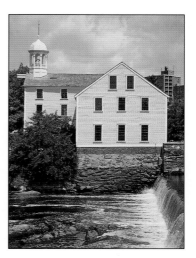

**OLD SLATER MILL**
67 Roosevelt Ave.
Pawtucket, RI 02862
401-725-8638
*www.slatermill.org*
NPS

The two-story wooden Slater Mill, built by the firm of Almy, Brown, and Slater in 1793, was the first successful water-powered cotton-spinning factory in America. Slater Mill's architecture, its management style, and its employment of children and women as mill operatives established the pattern used in numerous other mills in New England, including those in Lowell. The mill produced cotton until 1905. In 1933 the Old Slater Mill Association acquired the building. In 1955, after restoring it to its 1930 appearance, the association opened a museum in the historic building.

# Wesleyan Chapel, Women's Rights National Historical Park

## Seneca Falls, N.Y.

### Seeking Equal Rights

T he first women's rights convention ever to be held in the United States occurred in 1848. Elizabeth Cady Stanton, who spearheaded the organizing efforts for the meeting, set the tone for the occasion when she stated: "A new era is dawning upon the world,...when woman yielding to the voice of the spirit within her will demand the recognition of her humanity, when her soul, grown too large for her chains, will burst the bands around her...." It was at the Wesleyan Chapel in Seneca Falls, New York, on July 19 and 20, 1848, that more than 300 men and women assembled to consider the issues of women's social, educational, economic, religious, and legal rights.

It was not an accident that the first women's rights convention occurred in 1848. In the immediately preceding years there had been the first stirring of women's organized efforts to seek equitable pay in the workplace, and 1841 witnessed the first graduation of women from

*Elizabeth Cady Stanton (above), who served for fifty years as a brilliant intellectual leader of the woman's suffrage movement, moved to Seneca Falls with her husband and three small children in 1847. In the fifteen years she lived in this two-story house (right), she raised seven children; constantly wrote articles, speeches, and letters about women's rights; and tirelessly engaged in efforts to change public attitudes toward women.*

a full college course. Reform fervor was sweeping the world, not just the United States. In May 1848 the French government abolished slavery on Martinique, a Caribbean island that was a French colony, and on July 3, 1848, just prior to the women's rights meeting, the Dutch West Indies abolished slavery.

The organizers' choice of Seneca Falls, New York, for the meeting location was based in part on its proximity to the homes of key leaders. Located on the Seneca River, Seneca Falls was connected by way of the Cayuga and Seneca Canal to the Erie Canal, which was ten miles to the northeast. The village served as the commercial center for a rich agricultural area, and flour mills were one of its major industries. Additionally, there were saw and textile mills making use of the power provided by the river. Since Seneca Falls was next to a canal, a railroad line, as well as an east-west turnpike, it was an accessible location for a convention.

For several decades prior to 1848, Seneca Falls had been a gathering place for various reform causes such as antislavery and temperance, both of which had a relationship to women's rights. The antislavery cause, or abolitionist movement as it was frequently called, addressed the question of basic human rights for all men, which in the minds of some meant that women had rights, too. The temperance movement, while focusing on ending the use and abuse of alcohol, was also concerned with the injustices that many women, with no legal rights, experienced at the hands of alcoholic husbands. This section of New York state was also the scene of numerous religious revivals, which emphasized not only a person's spiritual state but also the importance of the individual in such endeavors as promoting public education and reducing the consumption of alcohol. In 1848 the Wesleyan Chapel in Seneca Falls was the site of the Union Temperance Society meeting, and in June there was a gathering in Seneca Falls of Freedmen, representatives of a growing free black population who were advocating an end to slavery in the United States.

The two principal organizers of the Seneca Falls Women's Rights Convention were Elizabeth Cady Stanton and Lucretia Mott. Stanton was a well-educated young woman who read extensively from her father's library and graduated from Troy Female Seminary. Her cousin, Garrit Smith, introduced her to the antislavery

*Lucretia Mott, who was a mentor to many young women in the women's rights movement, dressed in plain Quaker attire, including a bonnet and a shawl. Quaker women wore shawls instead of coats because of their simplicity.*

# Wesleyan Chapel, Women's Rights National Historical Park

Seneca Falls, NY 13148
315-568-2991
*www.nps.gov/wori/*
NRIS No. 91000342
NPS

**DATE BUILT**
1843; NPS made the preserved remnants a memorial park in 1993

**ORIGINAL OWNER**
Seneca Falls Wesleyan Methodist Church

**SIGNIFICANCE**
On July 19, 1848, more than 300 people assembled at the Wesleyan Chapel in Seneca Falls, New York, for the first women's rights convention ever held in the United States, a meeting that produced "The Declaration of Sentiments," a document that set the agenda that would guide the women's rights movement for the next century. In 1980 the National Park Service established the Women's Rights National Historical Park, which preserves and interprets the key sites and buildings associated with this meeting.

reform movement and to his work in sheltering fugitive slaves. While visiting Smith, she not only met fugitive slaves but also her future husband, Henry Stanton, a noted abolitionist.

Lucretia Mott, who was twenty-two years older than Stanton, had been raised in a Quaker home in which her parents were active participants in a variety of reform movements. She received a good education by the standards of the day and became a teacher. She soon met and married. After the death of her first child, she became increasingly involved in her Quaker congregation. In 1821 the Quaker meeting officially recorded her as a minister. This gave her speaking experience that was unavailable to most women at this time. As a mother of six children, a minister, and a leader in reform organizations, she had a very busy life.

In 1837 Mott helped to organize the Anti-Slavery Convention of American Women. This subsequently led to her attending the 1840 World's Anti-Slavery Convention in London, where she met Stanton, who was accompanying Henry Stanton, whom she had just married. While taking walks in London, the two women talked about the discrimination they felt at having to sit in a separate area behind a curtain at the Anti-Slavery Convention and not being able to participate in the proceedings. Mott and Stanton resolved that there was a need to hold a convention and to form a society to advance the rights of women.

Stanton, the major intellectual force behind the idea of the women's rights convention, was unable on her return from London to organize a convention because of her pregnancies and pressing household duties. Thoughts of planning a women's rights convention had to be postponed. Between 1842 and 1859, she had seven children. In 1847 the Stantons moved from Boston to Seneca Falls. Stanton missed the stimulation of urban life and her contact with reformers. She felt isolated and bogged down with domestic chores.

During her first year in Seneca Falls, Stanton became acquainted with some of her Irish immigrant neighbors and was often called upon to assist in solving their various domestic problems. She saw firsthand the anxieties and difficulties of poor women trying to hold families together with little control over their own lives or the resources of their households. While recognizing many aspects of women's inequality, Stanton focused her attention on seeking passage of a married women's property rights law.

In July 1848, when Lucretia Mott came from Philadelphia to the Seneca Falls area to visit her sister, Martha Wright, and to attend the Yearly Meeting of Friends in Western New York, she had an opportunity to get together with Stanton. Jane Hunt arranged the meeting. Hunt, a Quaker who grew up in Philadelphia, had married a Quaker businessman in 1845 and had moved to Waterloo, New York, just four miles up the river from Seneca Falls. On or about July 9, Hunt invited Stanton and Mott, along with Mott's sister and Mary Ann M'Clintock, who also had Quaker roots in Philadelphia, to tea at her home. Recalling this little gathering, Stanton later wrote that she had "poured out the torrent of my long-accumulating discontent with such vehemence and indignation that I stirred myself, as well as the rest of the party, to do and dare anything." The upshot of their discussion over tea was to place a notice in the local newspaper calling for a convention to discuss women's rights issues.

After deciding to hold a convention, the organizers had only a week to plan the agenda. Three days before the convention, they met again, this time at Mary Ann M'Clintock's home, a two-story brick house with a white front door and chimneys at either end, also located in Waterloo. It was there in the front parlor, seated around a mahogany center table, that they considered their past experiences with antislavery and temperance conventions and selected practices that seemed appropriate for a women's rights meeting.

*From 1849 to 1855 Amelia Bloomer edited and published* The Lily, *a newspaper "Devoted to the Interests of Woman," in Seneca Falls. Bloomer advocated many reforms, especially temperance and the wearing of loose-fitting women's clothing, such as pantaloons, which allowed freer movement and were healthier than tight corsets. The pantaloons she advocated soon became known as "bloomers" in her honor.*

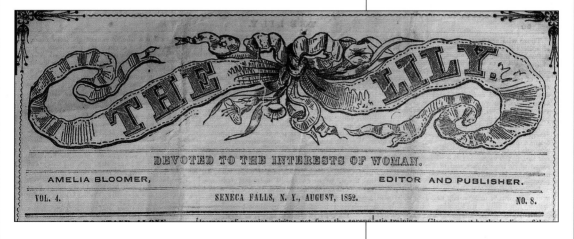

THE LILY.

DEVOTED TO THE INTERESTS OF WOMAN.

AMELIA BLOOMER,                                        EDITOR AND PUBLISHER.

VOL. 4.                     SENECA FALLS, N. Y., AUGUST, 1852.                     NO. 8.

*The sheet music for "We'll Show you when we come to Vote" shows women voting at a ballot box marked "For Ladies." The box is plastered with political signs, including "Vote For Susan B. Anthony For President." Social movements commonly inspire songs that support their causes, and the woman's suffrage movement was no exception.*

Prior to the meeting at M'Clintock's home, Stanton had drafted the Declaration of Sentiments using the Declaration of Independence as a model. The document affirms that all men and women are created equal. After stating that history shows repeated instances of men inflicting injuries on women, the declaration calls for "facts to be submitted to a candid world," one that would be fair and impartial. Instead of grievances against King George, the Declaration of Sentiments enumerates the inequalities between men and women, beginning with the fact that women were not allowed to vote and continuing with inequities such as women's limited access to education and employment opportunities. The declaration concludes with a stirring affirmation: "Firmly relying upon the final triumph of the Right and the True, we do this day affix our signatures to this declaration."

Although Mott and Stanton did not anticipate a very large turnout due to the short notice and the fact that it was a busy time in the farming community, they were amazed at the crowd of over three hundred. Charlotte Woodward, who was only nineteen in 1848 and was the only one of the one hundred signers of the declaration who lived to see the passage of the women's suffrage amendment in 1920, described the wagon loads of women coming from all parts of the county and forming a procession as they approached Seneca Falls on that summer morning.

The original plan had been for the first day to be for women only. However, so many men had come that the organizers decided to allow men to attend. They felt it appropriate to have a man preside and so asked James Mott, Lucretia's husband, to be the moderator. After calling the convention to order, Mott called on Elizabeth Cady Stanton to state the purpose of the convention. Mott then urged the women present to overcome their past training and societal restraints and participate in the debate over the many inequalities facing women. Stanton read the Declaration of Sentiments. The assembled discussed the various petitions, recommended some changes, adopted the final version, and later circulated papers to obtain signatures of support. One hundred people signed the declaration, sixty-eight women and thirty-two men.

The convention also included speeches by Stanton, Mott, M'Clintock, and Frederick Douglass, a freed slave who had become a leading abolitionist and advocate of women's rights. A key component of the convention was consideration of eleven resolutions aimed at addressing the inequities, such as denying women equal educational opportunities, that had been identified in the declaration. All resolutions passed unanimously, except the ninth resolution, which Stanton had written and which called for the vote for women. The suffrage resolution evoked considerable debate. Mott opposed it for fear that it would make the reformers look "ridiculous" and thus undermine the other resolutions. However, Douglass eloquently supported Stanton's call for women's suffrage and it ended up passing by a small majority.

The inside cover of this scrapbook belonging to Mary Anthony, the younger sister of Susan B. Anthony, contains the portraits of eleven leaders of the women's rights movement. From 1892 to 1901, Mary Anthony saved clippings, convention programs, and other material that documented the activities of the women's movement.

*Encircling the picture of Elizabeth Cady Stanton on this campaign button are the words "Equal Rights for Women" and "Harlem Equal Rights League." In 1890, as president of the National American Woman's Suffrage Association, Stanton used buttons, banners, and rallies to involve women in the cause of women's rights at the state level.*

The final business of the convention was the appointment of a small group, including Mary Ann M'Clintock and Elizabeth Cady Stanton, to prepare the proceedings of the convention for publication. This they did, and a published report of the convention appeared the following year and contained a summary of the meeting as well as the entire Declaration of Sentiments with the one hundred names of those supporting it and all of the resolutions.

Most of the newspapers that covered the event described the convention in sarcastic and negative terms. The signers of the Declaration found themselves the targets of ridicule. The attacks on some were so unrelenting that they withdrew their support from the cause of women's rights. Only the antislavery, abolitionist newspapers defended the goals of the convention.

The long-term importance of the Seneca Falls Convention rests in its direct exposure of the social, political, educational, economic, and religious institutions that restricted the lives of women. The Declaration of Sentiments became one of the founding statements of American feminism. It set the vision and the course for reform.

One of those who heard of the path-breaking convention and who subsequently claimed its goals as her own was Susan B. Anthony. Although she was not present at the Seneca Falls Women's Rights Convention in 1848, she followed developments in the emerging movement with great interest. In 1851 she finally met Elizabeth Cady Stanton. The two became a formidable team in the campaign for woman's suffrage. Anthony was the primary organizer, and Stanton was the sage thinker.

Anthony led by her actions. In 1872 she walked to the polls and voted in the Presidential election. She was hoping to prove that the recently passed Fourteenth and Fifteenth Amendments that gave the vote and the rights of citizenship to the freed slaves should also be applied to women. However, a U.S. Deputy Marshal arrested her in the parlor of her home for her illegal act and a judge fined her $100, which she refused to pay; her strategy being that a court trial would allow her to press the government for clarification of her arrest and fine. But the

U.S. Court, made no effort to enforce the payment of the fine, and as a result Anthony was unable to take the case to the Supreme Court as she had hoped.

Anthony died fourteen years before the passage in 1920 of the Nineteenth Amendment, giving women the right to vote. However, she played a pivotal role in laying the foundation for the victory. In February 1906, just two months before her death, she attended her last women's suffrage convention and in her message to the assembled she gave the rallying cry, "Failure is impossible."

Indeed, many of the women who gathered in Seneca Falls in 1848 believed that right was on their side and were determined to persevere in the long struggle to secure educational, social, economic, and legal rights for women. To preserve the buildings associated with the first women's rights convention and to commemorate the place where this struggle began, the National Park Service in 1980 established the Women's Rights National Park. The park consists of a little over four acres with several scattered properties. The focus of the park is the site of the Wesleyan Chapel, where there is now a memorial, and Declaration Park.

The site of the Wesleyan Chapel is centrally located on Bayard Street, one of the main thoroughfares of Seneca Falls, close to the Seneca River. Between the site of the Wesleyan Chapel and the Visitors Center is

# A Call to the Convention

 *This notice appeared in the July 11, 1848, issue of the* Seneca County Courier. *Newspapers offered one of the surest means of spreading the word in this rural county about the unconventional plan of bringing women together to discuss their social, civil, and religious conditions and rights.*

"WOMAN'S RIGHTS CONVENTION— A convention to discuss the social, civil, and religious condition and rights of woman, will be held in the Wesleyan Chapel, at Seneca Falls, N.Y., on Wednesday and Thursday, the 19th and 20th of July, current; commencing at 10 o'clock AM. During the first day the meeting will be exclusively for women, who are earnestly invited to attend. The public generally are invited to be present on the second day, when Lucretia Mott, of Philadelphia, and other ladies and gentlemen, will address the convention."

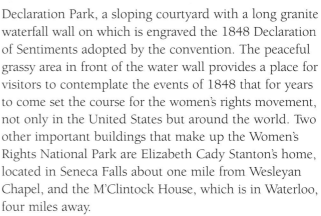

Declaration Park, a sloping courtyard with a long granite waterfall wall on which is engraved the 1848 Declaration of Sentiments adopted by the convention. The peaceful grassy area in front of the water wall provides a place for visitors to contemplate the events of 1848 that for years to come set the course for the women's rights movement, not only in the United States but around the world. Two other important buildings that make up the Women's Rights National Park are Elizabeth Cady Stanton's home, located in Seneca Falls about one mile from Wesleyan Chapel, and the M'Clintock House, which is in Waterloo, four miles away.

The most significant of these places for the commemoration of women's rights is the site of the Wesleyan Chapel, where the convention took place. Yet the historic building no longer stands. By 1980, when the Congress passed legislation to establish the Women's Rights National Historical Park, it had been last used as a laundromat and bore no resemblance to the church that the Wesleyan Methodists had sold in 1871. Over the years the building had also been used as an opera house, a furniture store, a theater, and a car dealership. Only scant written descriptions of the chapel as it existed in 1848 exist, and there are no pictures. But it is known that the chapel was only five years old at the time of the Women's Rights Convention, that it was a plain brick structure about forty-three feet wide and sixty-four feet long, and that the interior included a raised platform for the pulpit and galleries on three sides.

Despite the fact that only a few remnants of the Wesleyan Chapel remain, this is still the site, the ground on which the crucial 1848 women's rights convention took place. Because of the special importance attached to this place, the National Park Service struggled to salvage the two side walls and part of the roof, all that remains of the

*Elizabeth Cady Stanton (seated) and Susan B. Anthony enjoyed a fifty-year collaboration that brought together Stanton's speaking and writing skills and Anthony's organizational abilities and willingness to travel. They were very different people, Stanton funloving and Anthony stern, but they shared a passion for improving the conditions of American women.*

original building. Desiring to commemorate this place with more than a plaque, the National Park Service in 1987 held a design competition for a memorial for the Wesleyan Chapel. The winning design consisted of a simple structure the size of the original building, covered but open on the sides, that incorporates the few remaining fragments of brick wall and roof beams. This memorial stands as a reminder that women's struggle for equal rights continues to this day in the tradition of those who gathered at the Wesleyan Chapel in Seneca Falls in 1848.

## RELATED SITES

### M'CLINTOCK HOUSE

14 East Williams Street
Waterloo, NY
315-568-2991
*www.cr.nps.gov/nr/travel/
pwwmh/ny11.htm*

The M'Clintock House, where the women's rights advocates met on Sunday morning, July 16, 1848, to consider the agenda for the first conven-

tion, is a modest colonial revival two-story brick home. It is similar to numerous other homes built in the nineteenth century, yet it holds a special place in women's history because a small group of women, including Stanton, Mott, and M'Clintock, adopted a vision here and developed a plan for achieving women's rights.

### SUSAN B. ANTHONY HOUSE

17 Madison Street
Rochester, NY 14608
585-235-6124
*www.susanbanthonyhouse.org*
NHL

For forty years Anthony lived with her sister Mary on Madison Street in this two-story red-brick house in a middle-class neighborhood. This was not only her home but also her political head-quarters, where she held numerous meetings to plan strategy with the key leaders of the suffrage movement. Her house is now a museum and features many of her personal items, such as her desk, typewriter, her luggage, and many photographs.

*Anthony lived in this house in Rochester, New York, which is part of The Susan B. Anthony Preservation District. This nine-block area is one of the few nineteenth-century middle-class neighborhoods in the country that remains intact.*

# United Charities Building

## New York, N.Y.

### Women Advocating Reform

On March 6, 1893, the *New York Daily Tribune* carried a story on the opening and dedication of the United Charities Building. The headline read, "Charity's Fine Temple." More than 3,000 people attended and toured the new building. *The New York Times,* which also covered the event, described the building as a place where any applicant for relief could apply with the assurance that, if deserving, all the resources that the charities of New York had to offer would be provided. The building had a prestigious location on Park Avenue South near Gramercy Park and boasted modern and efficient offices. But it was the imposing structure, designed in the Renaissance Revival style, complete with arches and decorative detail, that conveyed to all who viewed it the importance and dignity of charity organizations.

*An organizer of charity societies, Josephine Shaw Lowell (above) had an astute mind for analyzing the root causes of poverty. For twenty-five years she was the guiding force of the New York Charity Organization, one of the groups responsible for building the United Charities Building (right).*

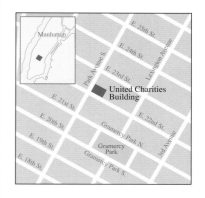

As the headquarters for a number of influential women's reform groups, the handsome United Charities Building stands as a testament to the growing maturity in the late nineteenth century of women's social service efforts. From the colonial period on, many women had assumed individual responsibility to help those in the community who were destitute. Women in the early nineteenth century went further: while acting within the narrow confines of "acceptable female behavior," they formed small local organizations such as orphan and benevolent societies to alleviate the suffering and misery of the outcasts of society and the poor. By the end of the nineteenth century, women's concern for those in need took the form of national reform organizations whose pioneering efforts promoted federal policies to deal with such problems as child labor.

The broad reform movement that swept the country in the late nineteenth and early twentieth centuries, often called the Progressive Era, sought in a wide variety of ways to preserve human values in an increasingly urban and industrial age. While women participated in many facets of the reform efforts of the Progressive Era, from working to get playgrounds in poor neighborhoods to advocating better housing, two areas where women provided exceptional leadership were in the united charity movement, which formed umbrella structures to foster coordination between the growing numbers of charity organizations, and in the establishment of settlement houses, where middle-class reformers lived in overcrowded, immigrant neighborhoods and led urban reform efforts. These represented two different approaches for dealing with the problems facing the poor, yet both had their roots in England and both enlisted educated young women in improving life in the slums and establishing a more just society.

The charity organization movement that began in the 1870s emphasized cooperation among the many benevolent organizations. A central organization allowed small charity societies— many of which specialized in dealing with one facet of assistance, such as aid to orphans or

*A group of Italian Americans stand outside their New York slum dwellings. The photographer, Jacob August Riis, gained a national reputation in 1890, when his pictures of slums and the abuses of lower-class urban life appeared in his groundbreaking book* How the Other Half Lives.

to the blind—to work together to provide more efficient support to those in need.

This united charity approach depended upon staff and volunteers who were well trained enough to be knowledgeable about the types of assistance provided by the various charity groups and confident about how best to conduct visits to the homes of those in need. The focus of the home visits was to discover the needs of the individual or family, to inform them of all of the assistance options, and to gather information about poverty-related problems. The united charity organizations did not provide direct relief but coordinated the aid provided by other groups. The New York Charity Organization Society was at the forefront of this movement and served as a model for similar organizations in other cities. The New York Charity Organization Society also led the way in moving beyond relief efforts to combine charity and reform by advocating legislation to address what it perceived to be the causes of the misery of the poor. Additionally, many of the umbrella charity organizations, like the one in New York, established incentives for individuals in need to exercise independence by learning skills and setting goals for themselves.

The workers from the charity organization societies who visited the needy in their homes were the forerunners of social service caseworkers. They gathered information and statistics into case files that were subsequently used to provide evidence for their reform agenda of decreasing the number of paupers by improving social conditions. This emphasis on data gathering and keeping case files led to the united charity organizations' work being called "scientific charity," or philanthropy. The concept of scientific charity developed in England in the 1850s and rested on the premise that the principles of science could be

*A drawing of the elegant lecture hall accompanied a* New York Daily Tribune *article about the opening of the United Charities Building. When John Stewart Kennedy, who provided the money for the building, rose to make his speech there was so much applause that he had to wait a full minute before beginning.*

THE MEETING IN THE LECTURE HALL.

applied to solve social concerns such as the elimination of poverty and other problems associated with the rapid changes brought about by the growth of industry and cities. This was the beginning of what is today called the social sciences, the identification and study of social issues and problems.

Although the initial impetus for a central building to house social welfare organizations came from men, the New York Charity Organization Society, which originated the idea of a charities building, was headed by a woman and women played a leading role in many of the social service organizations located in the United Charities Building. In 1890, John S. Kennedy, a wealthy businessman and a leader in several charity organizations, offered to undertake the construction of the United Charities Building. Not only would this donation of a central building make coordination easier but it helped solve the charity organizations' financial problem of meeting ever increasing rental costs. Kennedy stipulated that the owners of the building would be four charity organizations: the New York City Charity Organization Society, the Association for the Improvement of the Condition of the Poor, the Children's Aid Society, and the New York City Mission and Tract Society. These organizations would collectively have responsibility for the building with the expectation that they would rent the portions of the building they did not use to other charitable societies at rates considerably lower than those available elsewhere.

Kennedy's choice of R. H. Robertson, one of New York's leading architects, to design the building reflected how highly the charity organizations were regarded. The light gray limestone seven-story building features four distinct bands of decorative surface. For the main entrance, Robertson used a wide, two-story, semi-circular arched doorway with granite columns and ornamental patterns on either side. Above the entrance, on the third and fourth floors, are three connected semi-circular windows with rectangular decorative columns set into the wall on either side.

The most important room of the United Charities Building was the ground-floor assembly hall, entered directly from the entrance on 22nd Street. Its high walls have striking curved surfaces that connect to an elaborately detailed metal ceiling. Handsome rectangular pillars support arches that give the room an especially elegant

# United Charities Building

105 East 22nd Street
New York, NY 10010
*www.cr.nps.gov/nr/travel/pwwmh/
ny26.htm*
NRIS No. 85000661
NHL

**DATE BUILT**
1892

**ARCHITECT**
Robert Henderson Robertson

**SIGNIFICANCE**
The construction of the United Charities Building in 1892 was a milestone event in American philanthropy, for it brought together under one roof the headquarters of a wide variety of charitable organizations, many led by women, that provided social services to the poor and needy. In 1899 the National Consumers' League, one of the most influential of women's reform organizations, located its headquarters in the United Charities Building, which is still used as a headquarters office building for social service organizations.

appearance. The ornamental trim on semi-circular recessed panels includes decorative designs as well as plastic reliefs of the heads of children. A raised speaker's platform with a stately podium occupied one end of the room. Historic preservationists consider this meeting room to be an extraordinary survivor of the grand gathering places of the late nineteenth century. The building's interior retains the original oak paneling, glass doors with elaborate metal grillwork, and marble stairways with decorative iron railings.

The woman most influential in the early years of the united charity organization movement in New York City and in the building of the United Charities Building was Josephine Shaw Lowell. Born in 1843 to a privileged Boston family, she became a widow at twenty and moved to New York. After some experience visiting jails and poorhouses where those in desperate need could find a bed and a meal, she became convinced that charitable work needed to be coordinated in order to have the most impact on the poor. In 1876 she became the first woman to serve as a commissioner on New York's

*Graduate students in social work, mostly women, stand in front of the United Charities Building. The first formal study of social work began in 1898 with the New York Charity Organization, in connection with Columbia University. Originally called the New York School of Philanthropy, then the New York School of Social Work, it finally became the Columbia University School of Social Work in 1963.*

State Board of Charities, which had the official mandate of providing assistance to the poor. For thirteen years she prepared reports, gave lectures, and advocated a wide range of reforms, from removing children from jails to establishing separate jails for women and men. In 1882 she formed the Charity Organization Society of the City of New York with the express purpose of reducing waste and duplication among charity organizations. Adopting a business-oriented approach to charity, Lowell built a strong institutional base for the Charity Organization Society and was one of the first to conduct important research on poverty and develop the caseworker approach to social services.

The formidable assembly room of the United Charities Building was the nerve center of the charity activities. Since the major concept behind having one building that housed many charity groups was that they could work together, it was essential to have an impressive meeting room. Cooperating groups used it as a gathering place for policy discussions, and it was used for lectures by visiting scholars in the field of social work. Thus it was not surprising that the United Charities Society became the launching pad for the New York School of Philanthropy, now the Columbia University School of Social Work.

In addition to providing meeting space and head-quarters offices for the many different charity organizations, the United Charities Building served as a central place where those in need could apply for aid. Using a streamlined process designed to improve services to applicants, the staff and volunteers in the United Charities Building sought to match an applicant's particular problem

with the program most able to provide assistance. The coordinated relief efforts of the organizations in the building were most fully engaged when a tenement building collapsed, killing more than sixty people and tragically disrupting many families' lives.

The charity organization leaders placed considerable emphasis on maintaining careful records on each person helped, and these records became a key component in building a case for improved social conditions. Based on extensive research on the housing conditions in the slums of New York, relying in part on their own records, the Charity Organization Society developed in 1898 the Tenement House Exhibition. Using more than one thousand photographs, the exhibit exposed the shocking living conditions of thousands of New Yorkers and provided a plan for reform. A most compelling portion of the exhibit compared New York's housing for the working class with comparable housing in London and other major world cities and showed that while accommodations in New York cost more than elsewhere in the civilized world they were the most deplorable, characterized by awful darkness, terrible ventilation, limited toilets, and extreme overcrowding.

Displayed in a prominent Fifth Avenue building for two weeks, the Tenement House Exhibition was seen by middle- and upper-class people, many of whom expressed horror that such conditions existed in their city. With increased public awareness, the Charity Organization Society pressed forward and played a pivotal role in the passage in 1901 of the New York Tenement Act, which established standards for the construction of new tenements.

In addition to the work in the United Charities Building on social science research and social reform, there were also programs to encourage those in need with self-help measures. The emphasis placed on job training for the unemployed was reflected in the space in the United Charities Building that was set up as a cooking school.

From direct aid and training to innovative social science research and legislative reform efforts, Lowell was a guiding figure in the multifaceted activities undertaken in the United Charities Building. In 1912, seven years after Lowell's death, distinguished civic leaders and the mayor of New York were among five hundred guests who gathered in Bryant Park to dedicate a granite fountain to the memory of Josephine Shaw Lowell. This was the city's first public monument commemorating a woman. A nearby granite block with bronze lettering described Lowell's service to the state and city as "sincere, candid, courageous and tender" and commended her for "bringing help and hope to the fainting and inspiring others to consecrated labors." Seth Low, a former mayor of New York, spoke at the dedication and noted that Lowell's "real" memorial to the city was the Charity Organization Society, which within a few years of its founding was recognized as one of the nation's flagship charity organization societies. Lowell's philosophy of public aid stressed rehabilitation, not just relief efforts, and she developed disciplinary measures for those perceived to be lazy, reserving her support for the working, "deserving" poor.

Despite her achievements, the united charity movement and Lowell's leadership have not been without critics. Some of Lowell's contemporaries as well as some recent historians have seen the united charity movement as repressive and as an attempt at "social control," whereby the rich sought to ensure that the poor adopted moral values of hard work and individual responsibility. However, many of her goals, such as ending dependency on aid and social services, are very much part of the twenty-first century debate on poverty.

In contrast to the widespread network of organizations that were part of the united charity movement, the settlement house movement focused on establishing residences in needy neighborhoods. Educated middle- and upper-class reformers, mostly women, "settled" in the neighborhoods to become advocates and teachers, learning first hand about the conditions in poor areas and assisting their neighbors. Most settlement houses were in urban working-class neighborhoods, where the goal was often to help immigrants in adjusting to a new country.

Settlement house residents established neighborhood clubs and had special programs for young children of working mothers. Residents also taught classes in English, cooking, hygiene, and sewing. The settlement house leaders emphasized the arts by promoting music classes, art exhibits, concerts, and the celebration of festivals that preserved the ethnic identity of the immigrants. Hull House in Chicago, founded by Jane Addams in 1889, was one of the earliest and is today perhaps the best known of the settlement houses. But there were many others. By 1900 there were more than 100 settlement houses in the United States, and by 1910, more than 400.

Although settlement houses tried in many ways to be inclusive, they were not usually inclusive of all races. A segregated system of settlement houses evolved, with most organizations providing services for urban whites. Rural settlement houses and those aiding African Americans were the exception.

*An exhibit at the United Charities Building showcased affordable housing that was much improved thanks to the work of the building's charitable organizations. The caption below this longshoreman's kitchen boasted that "all rooms open on the street or on an interior park 100 feet wide and 250 feet long."*

The settlement houses became experimental laboratories for social research and reform, having a major influence on both those who gave and those who received assistance. Benny Goodman learned to play the clarinet at Hull House, and Frances Perkins, who in 1933 became the first woman to hold a cabinet level position, also lived and worked there. The connection between settlement houses and other reform efforts is well illustrated by the large number of settlement house residents who became national leaders in a wide range of institutions that sought to address issues of social justice.

A strong network of relationships existed between the settlement house workers and the advocates of the united charity movement. One of the early Hull House residents, Florence Kelley, subsequently became the head of the National Consumers' League, which some considered to be the most influential tenant in New York's United Charities Building. The National Consumers' League evolved from an investigative committee of the Working Women's Society, which was formed in 1890 and headed by Josephine Shaw Lowell and Mary Putnam Jacobi, a prominent reformer and physician. Using statistics gathered by the Charity Organization Society, they focused particularly on the abuses of child labor in sweatshops. The committee soon assumed the name of National Consumers' League and relied on the use of the buying power of shoppers, most of whom were women, to pressure employers to treat employees in a more humane way. Many historians consider the National Consumers' League to have been the single most effective lobbying agency during the Progressive Era for protective labor legislation for women and children. For thirty-four years, from 1898 to 1932, Florence Kelley served as executive director of the league, basing her successful leadership on her reform strategy of "investigate, educate, legislate, and enforce."

The United Charities Building was also the headquarters for the National Child Labor Committee and the Association for Labor Legislation, both of which collaborated with the National Consumers' League. In 1907, Lilian Brandt, a leader in the Charity Organization Society, wrote of the United Charities Building that "each succeeding year has added to the conviction that it embodies one of the wisest, most far-reaching benefactions of the period. The very lively personal intercourse among the leaders in the different organizations...could hardly have developed to such proportions without it, nor except for it could there be such effective formal co-operation as there is in so many ways." Especially for women in the late nineteenth and early twentieth centuries, the United Charities Building provided a place to pursue effective reforms.

*Big Log House, constructed in 1913 with forty-two-foot-long logs, was the first building of Pine Mountain Settlement School. Katherine Pettit, one of the two founders of the school, lived here with twenty-five children. The boys slept in a large attic room, the girls and staff stayed on the second floor, and a living room and kitchen occupied the first floor.*

system that tolerated violence against African Americans. An agitator who would not allow racial injustice to be ignored, she led the crusade against lynching of African Americans in the South. Despite her efforts, she was unable to persuade the suffrage organizations to take a stand against racism and lynching. It was not until 1930, a decade after women gained the vote, that Wells-Barnett convinced women to form the Association of Southern Women for the Prevention of Lynching. She died the following year. She lived from 1919 to 1929 in this house on one of Chicago's finest streets.

## PINE MOUNTAIN SETTLEMENT SCHOOL

36 Highway 510
Pine Mountain, KY 40810
606-558-3571, 606-558-3542
*www.pinemountainsettlement
    school.com*
NHL

Pine Mountain Settlement House, founded by Katherine Pettit and Ethel De Long, was one of the most important efforts to adapt the urban settlement house to a rural community with the goal of improving educational opportunities for children as well as adults. The campus, which eventually grew to include thirty-eight buildings, was the center for instruction in traditional subjects as well as classes in furniture making, home nursing, weaving, and raising

animals. Like the urban settlement houses, Pine Mountain Settlement School put an emphasis on the arts, and the residents worked to preserve regional ballads, folk songs, and dances and helped to promote a knowledge and appreciation of mountain heritage.

## IDA B. WELLS-BARNETT HOUSE

3624 South Martin Luther
    King Drive
Chicago, IL 60827
*www.cr.nps.gov/nr/travel/
    civilrights/il2.htm*
NHL

Using the power of the pen, Ida B. Wells-Barnett, who was born a slave in 1862 in Mississippi, worked all of her adult life to reform a judicial

*Ida B. Wells-Barnett lived in this handsome three-story Romanesque Revival stone residence in Chicago during the latter years of her life. Known primarily for her work protesting lynching, she also successfully integrated the woman's suffrage movement.*

# M. Carey Thomas Library

*Bryn Mawr, Pa.*

*Striving for
Equal Educational
Opportunities*

M. Carey Thomas (above), the dean and second president of Bryn Mawr College, improved the quality of education available to women. She made the library a centerpiece of campus life, and the central reading room (below) was, as Thomas had planned, as grand and impressive as any at Oxford or Harvard.

As President of Bryn Mawr College from 1894 to 1922, M. Carey Thomas insisted that the design for the college's new library embrace her vision of equal scholarly opportunities for women and the dignity and importance of research. She believed that buildings not only express the values of a community but that they also could influence behavior and aspirations. A grand, elegant library, according to Thomas, would stimulate intellectual pursuits and confirm Bryn Mawr's high scholarly standards. To convey her principles of academic excellence and the importance of original research, Thomas chose for the library a Gothic design with pointed arches, ribbed ceilings, and towers. The library, named the M. Carey

Thomas Library, was completed in 1907. Built of gray stone in the so-called collegiate Gothic style, it was Thomas's decision to model it after Oxford's Wadham College, built in 1630. The architecture of the library expressed her understanding of the dramatic and exhilarating aspects of exceptional scholarship.

As a champion of women's rights and women's education, Thomas was the first feminist to head a women's college. Other women had by this time headed women's colleges, but none had sought to challenge the accepted, yet restrictive, standards of female behavior as strongly as Thomas did. While seeking to offer women a high quality of education, as several other women's colleges were doing at that time, Thomas also strove to give her students the courage to break away from confining and traditional roles for women. She rejected the architectural design of some of the quality women's schools of the day because she did not want buildings that encouraged domestic female spaces or that restricted students' lives by placing them in overly protective environments. Instead she wanted an open campus with a quadrangle similar to those at Oxford and Cambridge; and she aspired to build a grand library that would be the centerpiece of the campus, graced with handsome dark wood, majestic windows, and large study tables.

The library was in no way to suggest a distinctly female space, just as the curriculum did not include courses geared to family or domestic interests. Thomas's goal was to maintain educational standards equal to those of the most respected male colleges and to challenge conventional notions about women's place in society. Not only did she establish entrance examinations as stringent as those at Harvard but she also required proficiency in Latin and Greek, subjects normally required only of men entering prestigious universities. She developed a rigorous curriculum based on clusters of courses taken in sequence and adopted Johns Hopkins University's use of the seminar method, which in contrast to lecture courses involved a small group of students meeting around a table for discussion with the professor.

Born in 1857 to a wealthy Quaker family in Baltimore, Thomas was blessed by having a mother, Mary Thomas, who was at the forefront of charitable undertakings and who did not advocate the commonly accepted view of a reserved and restricted life for girls. She allowed

her daughter to pursue her tomboy activities and her scholarly interests.

In the eighteenth century, there was a prevailing notion that women did not have the mental ability or stamina to undertake serious study, and that women should, at the most, receive only an elementary education. Following the Revolutionary War, however, the leaders of the country began to debate the question of female education. Some upheld the traditional view that women had limited capacity for reasoning and that the strain of serious study would be detrimental to their health and cause them to faint. Others affirmed girls' talents and the need to give them an opportunity to develop their individual gifts.

The final plans for the M. Carey Thomas Library show the stack area for books on the first floor and the formal entrance to the second floor, which leads into the spacious great hall that served as the reading room. The librarian at the time complained that the reading room was too large, larger than that of the British Museum.

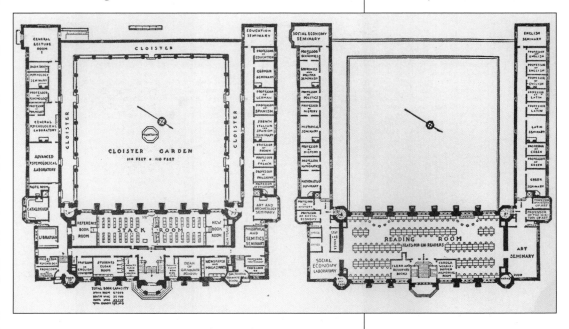

# M. Carey Thomas Library

Bryn Mawr College
Bryn Mawr, PA 19010
610-526-5000
*www.brynmawr.edu/Library/
  Exhibits/thomas*
NRIS No. 91002052
NHL

**ARCHITECTS**
Cope and Stewardson

**BUILT**
1904–1907

**SIGNIFICANCE**
As the dean and later president of Bryn Mawr College, M. Carey Thomas broke new ground in creating a campus that had as its centerpiece a collegiate gothic library that emphasized the importance of original research. At the time, such libraries were available at only a few of the most prestigious male schools.

Beneath the surface of the debate over female education was a tension between the need for women to be educated in order to be better mothers and supply a teaching force for the emerging democracy's schools, and a fear of what new rights and careers educated women might wish to pursue. Maria Weston Chapman, an abolitionist leader and a supporter of women's rights, wrote a satirical poem in the 1840s titled "The Times That Try Men's Souls" that captured the dilemma facing those who aimed at educating women to think but socializing them for a strictly traditional, prescribed sphere:

> Our grandmothers' learning consisted of yore
> In spreading their generous boards;
> In twisting the distaff, or mopping the floor,
> And obeying the will of their lords.
> Now misses may reason, and think and debate
> Till unquestioned submission is quite out of date.

Thomas fell squarely into the category of "misses" who thrived on an opportunity to "reason, and think and debate." She first attended a Quaker day school in her hometown of Baltimore and in 1873, at the age of sixteen, went to Howland Institute, a Quaker boarding school in New York not far from Cornell University. After completing her secondary education, she was eager to take the next step and go to college. As a young girl Thomas had dreamed of going to Vassar, a bold new women's college that had opened when the precocious Thomas was just eight years old, but as a teenager she wanted to go to Cornell. Her father, who held to the old view that it was not appropriate for women to pursue a higher education, opposed her attending Cornell. But her mother continued to be her staunch supporter.

Within the lifetime of Thomas's mother, female education in America underwent a major transformation. In the early nineteenth century numerous female seminaries sprang up around the country. These were preparatory schools that took the name "seminary" to convey the seriousness of the study and their commitment as a professional school to train young women to be mothers and teachers. Among the early seminaries that established strong academic programs that greatly increased the caliber of education available to women was Mount Holyoke Female Seminary, which was founded in 1837 by Mary Lyon and evolved into a college in 1888.

With opportunities for young women expanding, M. Carey Thomas had several choices in 1875 about where to go to college. She could have chosen an exceptional women's college such as Vassar, founded in 1866, or Smith College in Massachusetts, which was just opening that year. She also had the option of Oberlin College in Ohio, which was founded in 1833 and since 1837 had accepted all students, regardless of race or sex, or Antioch College, which became coeducational in 1852, or the University of Iowa, which in 1858 became the first state university to accept women. Instead, however, she was attracted to Cornell University, which was established as a male school in 1868 and in 1874 had just completed Sage Hall, a residence for women. Cornell's plan was to allow women to select their courses as freely as the male students and to adopt no restrictive practices toward female students.

## BRYN MAWR COLLEGE.

### EXAMINATION FOR MATRICULATION.

GREEK. *(Counted as three sections.)*

FIRST SECTION: GRAMMAR AND COMPOSITION.

SPRING, 1900.

*(One hour if all three sections are taken; one and a half hours if only one or two sections are taken at one time.)*

I. In the second prose passage (Xen. Anab. VII., 6, 43–44) decline in full ὁπλίτας, λαβών, Βασιλεῖ.

Give the principal parts of πέμπει, ἀποδώσειν, μένειν.

Conjugate in the mood and tense in which each is found: ὑπέσχετο, ἀχηχοε, ἔσται, ἀποθανοῖτο, εἴη.

Give all the infinitives of the verb from which διαβεβλημένος is formed.

Give the grammatical construction of ἀποδώσειν, ἀποθανοῖτο.

II. Translate into Greek:

Clearchus wished to have money so that he might raise an army, for war was more pleasant to him than peace.

The soldiers of Clearchus feared him more than they feared the enemy, and they say that Clearchus said that his soldiers must obey. So they followed him in the midst of danger because they thought him a good general, and whenever he led his men into battle, they fought nobly. Clearchus ruled them in order that he might not himself be ruled by them. With them he made war upon the Thracians and conquered.

42

*The first page of this 1900 exam required students to translate an English passage into Greek and conjugate Greek verbs. This examination, used as part of the entry requirements for Bryn Mawr College, illustrates well the high level of scholarship expected of incoming Bryn Mawr students.*

*A class of about twenty students works in a well-equipped laboratory conducting scientific experiments. M. Carey Thomas was not interested in creating feminine spaces; the quality of the library and the laboratories were of utmost importance to her.*

In 1875 Thomas enrolled as a junior at Cornell University with its first class of women. Two years later she graduated and applied to Johns Hopkins University but was denied access to the graduate seminars. A few years later she went to Europe to pursue her graduate studies, first in Germany and then in Switzerland where she received a Ph.D. in 1882 from the University of Zurich, becoming the first woman to receive its highest degree.

M. Carey Thomas's return to the United States came at the time that Joseph W. Taylor, a wealthy Quaker, had indicated his intention to bequeath funds to found a college that would provide young Quaker women with a quality education as well as training in orthodox Quaker traditions. Thomas approached the newly established board of trustees for Bryn Mawr, which included her father, about the possibility of becoming the college's first president. The Board, considering her age of twenty-seven and her lack of administrative experience, decided that James Rhoads, a retired physician, editor of the *Friends Review,* and a Haverford College trustee, should be president. They did, however, select M. Carey Thomas as the first member of the faculty and the dean; and the college opened for students in 1885. Ten years later, when Rhoads stepped down due to declining health, Thomas became the president of Bryn Mawr College.

Thomas's contribution in advancing educational opportunities for young women built on the work of many who had come before her. When Bryn Mawr was only an idea with no faculty, students, or buildings, Thomas, as the first dean, took an extended trip to visit the country's most outstanding schools for young women. After traveling to Vassar, Smith, Wellesley, and Radcliffe and talking to faculty and students, Thomas tried to sort out the best of the features of the women's colleges while also embracing the standards, curriculum, scholarship, and campus design of the men's schools. On June 7, 1884, she prepared a report to the president and trustees of Bryn Mawr College on the findings from her trip. She stated: "In none of the three colleges; Smith, Wellesley and Vassar, are there many professors who can lay claims to original scholarship, or who are fit to guide the students in original work." Operating on the principle that truth has no sex, Thomas wanted to create a campus environment that facilitated the pursuit of knowledge and was not bound by traditional notions of protecting female students.

Thomas's commitment to scholarship and to an education that had neither a male or female bias stood in contrast to the position of Sophia Smith, the founder of Smith College, who had stated: "It is not my design to render my sex any less Feminine, but to develop as fully as may be the powers of womanhood, and furnish women with the means of usefulness, happiness and honor, now withheld from them." Meanwhile, Thomas was joining with suffrage leaders to seek the vote for women. She served as president of the National College Equal Suffrage League for almost a decade. For thirty-six of the thirty-seven years that Thomas served as dean and then president of Bryn Mawr, women in the United States were not allowed to vote, an injustice that Thomas abhorred.

In keeping with Thomas's emphasis on the importance of original scholarship, her wish that faculty and students undertake individually designed research projects on facets of previously unexplored questions, she viewed the library, the center of research, as central to her dream for the campus. From 1885, when as dean she began hiring the first faculty for Bryn Mawr, she recruited many young men who had received graduate training in German universities that used the latest research methodologies. To emphasize her commitment

# Bryn Mawr's Plans Take Shape

M. Carey Thomas made this drawing of the Bryn Mawr campus around 1898. In 1895, Thomas invited Frederick Law Olmsted, the nationally renowned landscape designer, to visit Bryn Mawr to give advice on how best to proceed with the development of an expanded campus. Thomas, in consultation with the architects and Olmsted, decided that the library's placement should form an open quadrangle. The library entrance would be located opposite the tower of Taylor Hall, with the long, double dormitory, Pembroke East and West, forming a side of the quadrangle. Although Olmsted was essentially retired at this time, he played a major role in planning the Bryn Mawr campus, and in 1897 he offered to have the general plan for the campus lithographed. Thomas decided instead to make a sketch of the plan herself, a reduced version of which could be easily reproduced and used in fundraising.

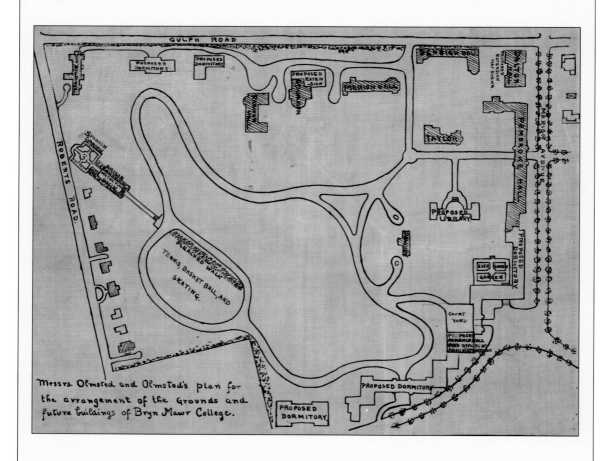

Messrs. Olmsted and Olmsted's plan for the arrangement of the Grounds and future buildings of Bryn Mawr College.

to original research, she reduced the faculty's teaching responsibilities to give them more time for their own scholarly work. She stressed the importance of seminar classes that offered students and faculty an opportunity to discuss the results of their individual research projects. To provide faculty with incentives to stay abreast of their fields, Thomas instituted graduate programs, the first within a women's college, in the humanities and the sciences. In 1915 she established the first graduate department for social work in the country.

During her tenure as president, she oversaw a far-reaching building campaign that included four residential halls, a science building, a gymnasium, and a library. Although construction on the library did not begin until 1904, Thomas began planning for it as early as 1895. In the 1897 general plan for the expansion of the Bryn Mawr campus, the proposed library was a key component in the creation of a collegiate quadrangle.

The completion in 1907 of the M. Carey Thomas Library marked the culmination of Thomas's efforts to raise the level of women's education and highlighted her twin goals of academic and architectural excellence. The library's gothic elements were all inspired by the buildings at England's most prestigious universities, Oxford and Cambridge. The entrance of the library was a copy of the one at Oriel College at Oxford and the main reading room was based on the dining hall of Oxford's Wadham College. In convincing the board of trustees of the value of original scholarship in a college for women, Thomas also convinced them of the importance of creating splendid spaces for living and studying that combined dignity with dramatic effects.

Built of gray stone with arches and towers, the library features a spacious great hall that served as an elegant reading room. With high ceilings and oak-paneled walls, the reading room has huge lead-paned windows that let in sunlight, creating a cathedral-like setting for the 134 tall study desks. The north and south wings, about two hundred feet in length and running parallel to each other, form two of the sides of the rectangular cloister. Some of the rooms in these wings originally contained collections of books on special topics; others were used as seminar classrooms or professors' studies. A covered passageway with vaulted ceilings and arches surrounds a grassy courtyard with a fountain in the center.

Thomas worked closely on the designs for the buildings with the Philadelphia architectural firm of Cope and Stewardson. Walter Cope, a young man whose sister had been in Bryn Mawr's first class and whose uncle was on the board of trustees, had traveled in Europe and was not only talented but had a cosmopolitan and sophisticated flair that appealed to Thomas. Stewardson had studied at the Ecole des Beaux-arts in Paris. The success of Cope and Stewardson's buildings at Bryn Mawr led to future commissions at the University of Pennsylvania, Princeton, and Washington University in St. Louis. The new "collegiate Gothic" style, initiated in the United States by Thomas, was spreading.

Thomas chose the quadrangles of men's schools as her models for the Bryn Mawr campus. She rejected Vassar's idea of safeguarding students in large communal, multifunctional buildings where they both slept and had classes, nor did she borrow Smith's tradition of creating small, domestic-style residential buildings called cottages that replicated family life. Thomas chose the quadrangle, where a number of exquisite buildings, with the majestic library as the centerpiece, surrounded a central lawn or large courtyard. The young women could move freely from large residential halls to the library and laboratories, just as men did at Harvard and Yale. This attitude toward student independence led Bryn Mawr to establish a system of student government in 1892, the first in an American women's college.

Although she was a Quaker, Thomas had had a strong love of drama and pageantry since childhood and did not espouse the plain clothes and modest lifestyle advocated by most Quakers. Her desire to create

*In this 1899 portrait by the American artist John Singer Sargent, M. Carey Thomas wears a richly colored academic robe as if she were royalty sitting on a throne. Bryn Mawr was Thomas's domain, and with determination and forethought she steered the course of the college toward a position of excellence in women's education.*

splendid spaces for studying and living, and her commitment to very high academic standards, often put her at odds with her board of directors. Under Thomas's leadership Bryn Mawr was gaining a national reputation for its rigorous standards, outstanding faculty, and brilliant students. Yet the trustees questioned her expensive building campaign and were disturbed that Bryn Mawr was moving away from its original intent of educating young Quaker women. However, Thomas argued that to build a first-class school they needed to draw on a larger pool of prospective students. In 1893, after some debate, the trustees voted to follow Thomas's direction and to broaden the college's mission beyond the Quaker community and make Bryn Mawr a non-denominational college. In 1897, just fifteen years after the college had accepted its first class of students, Bryn Mawr's entering class had thirty Episcopalians and twenty-four Presbyterians but only two Quakers.

Thirty-five years after Thomas's death and approximately sixty years after the building of the M. Carey Thomas Library, Bryn Mawr built a larger and much needed new library, the Miriam Coffin Canaday Library. In 1970, the college transferred the bulk of the holdings of the M. Carey Thomas Library to the new Canaday Library, leaving some of the art and archeology collection in the Thomas Library. Since the building of its third library, the Rhys Carpenter Library, Bryn Mawr has no longer used the M. Carey Thomas Library for any of its collections. Today the renovated Great Hall of the M. Carey Thomas Library is used for concerts, recitals, and symposia. Much of the area that once served as library stacks is now used for academic offices and classrooms. The renovations, however, made no changes in the grand spaces or the gothic details. Thomas's cremated remains lie in the cloistered courtyard under a commemorative plaque.

The M. Carey Thomas Library captures well the legacy of Thomas. It stands as an impressive reminder of her work to enable young women in the late nineteenth and early twentieth centuries to have access to an academic program that emphasized original research, offered graduate degrees, provided an environment that respected student's independence, and rivaled the best male colleges in the country.

*Students wearing white graduation dresses, black academic capes, and traditional mortarboard hats leave in double lines from the M. Carey Thomas Library during commencement ceremonies. The grand gothic entrance of the library and the arched lead-paned windows of the great hall can be seen in the background.*

## EMMA WILLARD HOUSE

131 South Main Street
Middlebury, VT 05753
802-443-3000
NHL

As Emma Willard's residence from 1809 to 1819, this house commemorates her initial efforts in 1814 to establish a school to provide exceptional high-school education to women and prepare them to become school teachers. In 1821, with the support of $4,000 raised from local taxes, Willard founded Troy Female Seminary in Troy, New York. By 1831, Troy Female Seminary had more than one hundred boarding students and more than two hundred day students. The curriculum for the advanced students included history, literature, trigonometry, chemistry, German, French, and Greek. Many of the most influential women of the nineteenth century, including Elizabeth Cady Stanton, attended Troy Female Seminary. The building now houses the admissions office for Middlebury College.

## PRUDENCE CRANDALL HOUSE

Junction of State Routes 14 and 169
Canterbury, CT 06331
860-546-9916
www.chc.state.ct.us/Crandall%20Museum.htm
NHL

In 1832 Prudence Crandall opened a girls' school in her home that was to become the

In 1831 Prudence Crandall purchased this large house for the operation of her school, the Canterbury Female Boarding School. The rooms were used in a flexible manner, for both living and learning. She taught reading, writing, arithmetic, English grammar, geography, history, chemistry, astronomy, and moral philosophy and charged $25 a quarter for tuition and room and board.

first in the country to admit an African-American girl. A teacher and an abolitionist, Crandall counted among her friends and supporters the noted abolitionist and newspaper publisher William Lloyd Garrison. Because of mob protests and harassment from the courts, Crandall was forced to close her school in 1834. But her fight to provide a school for African-American girls received national attention and brought needed visibility to the issue of education for African-American women.

Prudence Crandall left the town of Canterbury soon after the school closed, but she continued to be an advocate for educational opportunities for African-American girls. In her later years she moved to Kansas, where she started a school that served American Indians.

## OBERLIN COLLEGE

173 West Lorain Street
Oberlin, OH 44074
440-775-8121
www.oberlin.edu
NHL

The acceptance of four women at Oberlin College in 1837 marked the beginning in the United States of co-education at the college level. None of Oberlin's early buildings is still standing; but an elm tree from the 1830s marks the location of the early campus.

Although the first women students at Oberlin took a less rigorous course of study than the men, by 1841 Oberlin graduated its first woman from the "full course." Oberlin remained the only coeducational college in the country from 1841 until 1853, when Antioch College, also in Ohio, was founded and admitted men and women.

## OLD MAIN

Vassar College
Poughkeepsie, NY 12604
800-437-7000
NHL

The founders of Vassar college, one of the first women's colleges to offer to women the same education that was available at the better men's colleges, enlisted the nationally noted and fashionable architect James Renwick to design Old Main, the grand central building, which was built from 1861 to 1865.

Inspired by the ornate French chateaus and drawing on his experience building asylums, he created a gigantic, grand building. The central part of the building was a four-story pavilion with a handsome dome. The pavilion had large imposing parlors, a grand dining room, lecture rooms, a library, music room, an enormous chapel that would seat 600 people, majestic stairways, and the President's and senior professors' accommodations. The interior of the extensive three-story wings

on either side of the central pavilion was plain, in contrast to the central portion. The wings contained the modest living quarters for the students and most of the teachers.

The philosophy behind Old Main was to create a communal environment that would both protect and allow constant supervision of the students. In 1865 the first class of 353 young women arrived at Old Main, which was one fifth of a mile long and the largest building in the United States at the time.

*For the first thirty years of its existence, Old Main was the primary building on the Vassar campus. It housed classrooms, the library, the dining hall, and the residences for both faculty and students. Today the Vassar campus has numerous buildings, and Old Main is one of nine residence halls.*

# Asilomar Conference Center

*Pacific Grove, Calif.*

*Breaking Professional Barriers*

*Born in 1872 in San Francisco, Julia Morgan (above) had a brilliant career as one of this nation's earliest and most prolific women architects. When she died at eight-five, she left a legacy of hundreds of buildings, large and small, in which she skillfully combined creative design and the latest technology.*

Julia Morgan, a determined, proficient, and brilliant architect, had considerable experience in breaking professional barriers during her forty-five-year career as the designer of more than 800 residential and institutional buildings. She was the first woman to graduate in architecture from the Ecole des Beaux-arts in Paris and the first woman in California to pass the certification examinations and receive an architect's license. Yet many people are unfamiliar with her work. Although she had close colleagues and friends, she avoided large social events and never sought the limelight. She shunned reporters who wished to interview her, discouraged publication of feature articles about her work, and destroyed all of her papers when she retired in 1951.

Rarely have women entered into fields from which they were previously excluded without benefit of supporters and mentors. In Morgan's case, her parents enjoyed walks with their children around the city, investigating construction sites. Morgan became interested and curious about the challenges of construction. Her parents wanted to broaden their children's opportunities by supporting them, daughters as well as sons, in studying both at the undergraduate and graduate level. Further family support came from Pierre LeBrun, a well-known New York architect and the husband of one of Morgan's cousins. On several family visits to the East Coast during her formative years, Morgan became fascinated by LeBrun's architectural work. Over the years he advised and encouraged her.

Morgan's chief academic mentor was Bernard Maybeck, an engineering professor at the University of California at Berkeley. In 1890, when Morgan was eighteen and deciding on where to attend college, the only

*The interior of Merrill Hall, an auditorium that seats 1,000 people, has exposed supporting beams, long rows of arched gothic windows, and large light fixtures hanging from the ceiling. The last structure Morgan built at the Asilomar Conference Center, Merrill Hall is also the most sophisticated and complex on the grounds.*

school that offered training in architecture and that also admitted women was the Massachusetts Institute of Technology (MIT), which had opened its doors to women four years earlier. Morgan chose to stay in her home state, however, and went to the University of California at Berkeley, where she majored in engineering. She was the only woman in many of her classes. Although Berkeley did not at that time have a program in architecture, Maybeck had studied at the Ecole des Beaux-arts, an internationally renowned school of architecture that had a very competitive and rigorous course of study. Yet, Maybeck was in no way tied only to classical architecture. He was among a small group in the Bay Area of California who had become attracted to the architectural aspects of the arts and crafts movement, which advocated simpler styles, construction that highlighted the work of skilled craftsmen, and buildings that fit into the natural environment. Morgan received her first introduction to the arts and crafts movement from Maybeck. After graduation from the University of California, Morgan worked for a year in Maybeck's private architectural firm. During this year, Maybeck learned that the Ecole des Beaux-arts was considering accepting women into its programs and he encouraged Morgan to pursue formal architectural studies in France.

Morgan knew that achieving her dream of becoming an architect would not be easy. She set two goals: to get the best architectural education possible and to open her own architectural office. With Maybeck's encouragement and her family's support, she spent six years, from 1896 to 1902, studying in Paris accompanied first by a friend and later by her brother. Her first years were spent learning French and taking preparatory classes, and it was not until two years later, in October 1898, that she successfully passed the entrance examinations for the Ecole des Beaux-arts. The *San Francisco Examiner* carried the headline: "California Girl Wins High Honor, Miss Julia Morgan in the Ecole des Beaux-arts, First Woman who Has Entered the Architecture Department Is a Graduate of Berkeley."

As a student at the Ecole des Beaux-arts Morgan mastered a wide range of historical styles, learned historical solutions to architectural problems, and acquired the ability to develop her own innovative designs. Much of the training at the Ecole des Beaux-arts involved the submission of architectural designs to various competitions. Morgan's first award came in 1900 in a competition in which contestants were to design a bell tower for the roof of a city hall. While at the Ecole she entered almost thirty competitions and received a number of medals.

It was in Paris that Morgan first met Phoebe Hearst, who would become one of her chief patrons. Hearst, a wealthy widow who in 1897 became the first woman Regent of the University of California, possessed a strong interest in architecture and in advancing the education and professional careers of young women. The occasion for their meeting was a visit that Hearst, along with Morgan's former professor, Maybeck, made to Paris to discuss a proposed design competition for Berkeley's master plan. They met with Morgan and heard of her loneliness and difficulties in gaining admission to the Ecole des Beaux-arts. Hearst was impressed by Morgan's determination and ambition, and the two became friends.

Returning to California in 1902, Morgan worked with architect John Galen Howard on two major buildings on the Berkeley campus, the Hearst Mining Building and the Greek Theater, both financed by Phoebe Hearst. Increasingly impressed with Morgan's

# Asilomar Conference Center

Pacific Grove, CA 93950
831-372-8016
*www.asilomarcenter.com*
NRIS No. 87000823
NHL

**DATE BUILT**
1913–1928

**ARCHITECT**
Julia Morgan

**SIGNIFICANCE**
The layout and design of the eleven historic buildings of the Asilomar Conference Center are excellent examples of how Julia Morgan, relying on native materials and quality workmanship, used the arts and crafts style to blend buildings with their environment.

work, Hearst encouraged her to open her own office and helped to steer clients her way. In 1919, much later in her career, Morgan wrote to Hearst expressing her appreciation for Hearst's generosity throughout Morgan's career: "So through it all is the thread of your kindness since those Paris days when you were so beautifully kind to a most painfully shy and homesick girl. My mother's and yours are the greatest 'faiths' put in me, and I hope you both know how I love and thank you for it."

Two early projects that helped to establish Morgan's reputation were the rebuilding of the Fairmont Hotel in San Francisco, which had been destroyed by the 1906 earthquake, and the construction of St. John's Presbyterian Church in Berkeley. With her design of St. John's Presbyterian Church, Morgan created a small but extraordinary building on a quite limited construction budget. The Presbyterian group wanted a simple economical building to use for Sunday School classes and planned to build the main church a few years later.

*A large gathering of men and women eat at long tables in the Crocker Dining Hall at the Asilomar Conference Center in 1922. Constructed in 1918, the dining hall exhibits many of the features of the craftsman style, such as the large redwood beams and central granite fireplace.*

AL CONVENTION CALIFORNIA
ASILOMAR, CALIF OCT 17-20-22

Using redwood, the cheapest building product then available in California, Morgan paid close attention to the effects of natural light in her design plans, drew on the simple quality of the arts and crafts principles, used a series of classical arches, incorporated narrow vertical windows reminiscent of sixteenth-century Gothic cathedrals, and integrated the English Tudor element of using special timbers as an outline on the exterior. She combined complex elements to create a simple form and an inexpensive but beautiful building.

The growth of women's organizations, the maturing of Morgan's architectural practice, and the increasing philanthropy of Phoebe Hearst all came together when Morgan received the commission to design a conference center for the YWCA. The national YWCA at this time was responding to the need across the country to provide low-cost housing and services for the flood of young single women moving to the cities to seek work. The YWCA recognized that with the increasing numbers of their "home-like" housing facilities there was a need for a leadership training center for the staff who ran the local YWCAs. Phoebe Hearst donated the land and recommended that Morgan be retained as the architect.

In 1912 Morgan accepted a commission to design a Young Women's Christian Association (YWCA) conference center on a spectacular site on the Pacific coast. Located near Monterey, California, the property included a pine forest that extended down to the white sand dunes of the beach. Morgan developed a plan that was both functional for the Y and also melded the buildings into the natural environment. Asilomar, which in Spanish means "refuge by the sea," was graced with both a handsome campus of buildings and a beautiful setting.

Morgan's work on designing the buildings for the Asilomar Conference Center spanned more than two decades. However, it was her first building, completed in 1913, that set the style. Featuring simple arts and crafts elements, Morgan used the natural products of the area, redwood and stone, and incorporated the structural material into the design by leaving the interior wooden studs and roof braces exposed. Following the principles of the arts and crafts movement, Morgan emphasized the connection between labor and art. Throughout the construction process, she made frequent trips to Asilomar and supervised the work of highly qualified artisans and skilled craftsmen. She developed a special rapport with the construction crews and had the ability to discuss with the plumbers, ornamental plasters, carpenters, and tile layers various problems and aspects of their work.

Taking into consideration the particular needs of the YWCA, Morgan envisioned the buildings of the conference center as functional yet coordinated with nature. Her layout placed the social hall, dining hall, auditorium, and chapel in a circular campus on the edge of the woods but sheltered from the ocean by the sand dunes. She placed the dormitories back in the trees. Built of redwood and concrete with granite stones covering the concrete supports and foundation, the first structure on the campus, originally the social hall and now an administrative building, has one large central rectangular room. Small offices, clubrooms, and restrooms were on

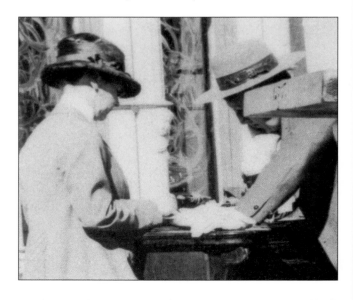

*Morgan draws on blueprints for the Hearst Castle as her client, William Randolph Hearst, the newspaper magnate, watches. This project was the most challenging and extensive of Morgan's career and included a main house with 38 bedrooms, several guest houses, gardens, pools, and terraces.*

either end, with balconies overlooking the large central room. The interior has exposed unpainted timber beams with open ceilings, a massive fieldstone fireplace, and numerous well-proportioned windows providing a grand view of the ocean. Five years after its completion, a bell tower was added to the roof of the social hall. The next building for the conference grounds was the chapel and then the dining hall. Finally, in 1928, Morgan designed the auditorium, Merrill Hall, which would seat a thousand people and which seemed to rise naturally out of the landscape.

Asilomar is possibly the largest institutional complex in the United States to be built in the arts and crafts style. In 1963, when the YWCA was unable financially to maintain the conference center, it became a part of the California State Park system. Although Morgan's most rustic dormitories, called "long tent-houses" because they had a long wooden frame and canvas walls, were torn down in the 1960s and early 1970s, her eleven most important structures are still standing. Those entrusted with the modernization of the conference center have been careful to retain the arts and crafts style and the harmony of the buildings with the landscape.

The success of Morgan's buildings at Asilomar helped to advance her career, and her firm began to hear from more potential clients. Located in the Merchants Exchange Building, one of San Francisco's early skyscrapers, Morgan's office had a large central drafting room that accommodated as many as a dozen architects and apprentices. A section of the drafting room also served as the library, where there were more than five hundred books related to architecture. In addition to the large drafting room, there was one small administrative office and one separate office for meeting privately with clients. Morgan ran a very efficient operation in which she expected everyone to work hard and to be as careful about details as she was. Yet she treated her staff as extended family, and in good years shared the profits with all employees, an unusual practice for architectural firms. As mentor to young women architects, Morgan helped to launch a number of women's careers.

Morgan closed her office in 1951 at the age of seventy-nine and died in 1957. She left a legacy of innovation in both the rough dark redwood of the crafts style and the smooth white sculptured forms of Mediterranean

*The Ecole des Beaux-arts in Paris awarded Morgan this medal for her entry in an architectural drawing competition. Students at the Ecole des Beaux-arts took examinations, but they also were expected to compete successfully in various kinds of design and drawing competitions.*

architecture. An engineer as well as an architect, she was one of the first to use reinforced concrete in domestic and public buildings. With great sensitivity to light and color, she was ahead of her time in her appreciation of the relationship of indoor and outdoor spaces, and used windows, lighting fixtures, decks, patios, and gardens to special effect. She had an exceptional feel for the needs and wishes of her clients and tried always to balance the standards of architecture she had learned in Paris with her understanding of the California landscape. In 1929 the University of California granted Morgan an honorary Doctor of Laws degree. The citation read: "Distinguished alumna of the University of California; Artist and Engineer; Designer of simple dwellings and stately homes, of great buildings nobly planned to further the centralized activities of her fellow citizens; Architect in whose works harmony and admirable proportions bring pleasure to the eye and peace to the mind."

## Morgan Writes about Her Exams at Ecole des Beaux-arts

 *Julia Morgan wrote this letter from Paris on November 14, 1898, to her cousins in Brooklyn Heights, New York. In the letter she describes the third time she took the oral examination to enter the Ecole des Beaux-arts.*

The judgement [result of examinations] was given today only, and I am the 13th—ten French and two foreigners—they take forty [thirty] in all. It's not much but has taken quite a little effort. If it had been simply for the advantages of the Ecole, I would not have kept on after M. Chaussemiche was arranged with, but a mixture of giving up something attempted and the sense of its being a sort of test in a small way, of work itself overcoming its natural disadvantages—made it seem a thing that really had to be won.

None of those had tried less than twice. Everybody takes defeat in the most cheerful way, for you are always in the majority.... The

oral examination broke down a hundred at least. It's the most trying ordeal for its simpleness.... There were thirteen examined before me the day I came up and everybody failed entirely—those big, strong fellows would get up, tremble, turn white, clutch their hands and seem to have no thinking power left.... When I was called there was a room full. I tried to pretend I was not afraid, and perfectly steady, and actually believed it until at the end of the first problem I discovered that my hand was rattling in the air, and the discovery so surprised me, I could not do any more mathematics—it was enough for a pretty good mark, but you see so many did nothing.

## HOLLYWOOD STUDIO CLUB

1215 Lodi Place
Hollywood, CA 90038
NPS

Mrs. Cecil B. DeMille, chairman of the Los Angles YWCA Building Committee Commission, contracted with Julia Morgan in 1923 to design a building to provide housing and recreational facilities for the numerous young women who were moving to Hollywood in hopes of establishing careers in the rapidly expanding movie industry.

Approximately ten thousand young women, including Marilyn Monroe, Donna Reed, and Kim Novak, were residents at one time or another at the Hollywood Studio Club. For this urban setting, Morgan used a Mediterranean style with white exterior surfaces, arches, and interior tiled floors.

## HEARST SAN SIMEON ESTATE

750 Hearst Castle Road
San Luis Obispo, CA 93452
805-927-2020
*www.hearstcastle.org*
NHL

A month after the death of Phoebe Hearst, her son, William Randolph Hearst, a wealthy publisher of newspapers and magazines, went to Morgan's office to discuss building a place of his own. He had chosen for his site a hilltop at San Simeon, located on the coast about

*Morgan's most involved and lengthy architectural project was the exotic Hearst Castle. Located on 127 acres, the estate includes a main house, numerous guest houses, gardens, pools, and terraces.*

two hundred miles south of San Francisco. From 1919 to 1938, Morgan took the train and spent most weekends at San Simeon designing and overseeing the construction of the massive and complex project that included a main building and numerous smaller buildings as well as several elegant pools and even a zoo.

The main building, often called the castle, has 165 rooms, all with architectural elements imported from around the world. A special challenge of the design of San Simeon was to create spaces appropriate for the display of antique furniture and rare art objects. While the San Simeon project involved many exotic and dramatic architectural styles, Morgan adhered to her crafts principles of employing highly

qualified artisans as tile designers, ironworkers, wood carvers, stone casters, and ornamental plasterers. Hearst Castle is no longer a private home; it is now operated as a museum by the California State Parks Department.

## HOPI HOUSE

Grand Canyon National Park,
    AZ 86023
928-638-7888
*www.cr.nps.gov/nr/feature/wom/
    2001/colter.htm*
NPS

Hopi House is one of four structures designed in the early twentieth century by Mary Colter for the National Park Service. It reflects her commitment to preserving Indian culture and creating architecture that is harmonious with the landscape. Hopi House embodies Colter's key ideas about architecture—that buildings should emerge out of their settings and should reflect the history and culture of the location. Colter did not try to create replicas of earlier buildings, but she did try to capture the essence of the past and express her extraordinary appreciation for Native American culture. Hopi House drew on the design of ancient Hopi dwellings, using log beams, stone, and adobe. The multi-story building featured flat rooftops that became the terraces for the story above. The building served as a museum, sales area, and residence for Native American artisans.

# Madam C. J. Walker Building

## Indianapolis, Ind.

### Succeeding as an Entrepreneur

*Known primarily as an exceptionally successful businesswoman, Madam C. J. Walker (above) was also a philanthropist and social activist. The Walker Theatre (below) was the center of African-American life and culture in segregated Indianapolis.*

A determined and innovative person with strong organizational and marketing skills, Madam C. J. Walker was at the forefront of the modern cosmetic industry and was one of the first women in modern America to establish her own business empire. At the National Negro Business Convention in 1912 she told the audience: "I am a woman who came from the cotton fields of the South. I was promoted from there to the washtub. Then I was promoted to the cook kitchen, and from there I promoted myself into the business of manufacturing hair goods and preparations. . . . I have built my own factory on my own ground." Walker was not only a successful self-made woman, she was a champion of African-American and women's rights and used her money in ways that advanced the cause of equality of opportunity.

After having founded the Walker Manufacturing Company in 1906 in Denver, Walker moved the operation to Indianapolis in 1910. In 1927, eight years after Walker's death, her daughter oversaw the construction in Indianapolis of the Walker Building, which served not only as the company's national headquarters, manufacturing site, and community cultural center but also as a testament to the vision and life of Madam C. J. Walker. The impressive structure reflected not only Madam Walker's personal achievement as a businesswoman but also her commitment to the employment of African Americans and her promotion of the arts in the African-American community.

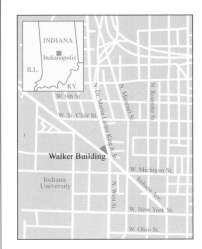

The four-story building had a triangular floor plan to adapt to the narrow angle at the intersection of two major avenues near the downtown commercial area. Built with steel and reinforced concrete, the exterior was finished in pressed pale yellow bricks with multi-colored terra-cotta borders around the first floor doorways and windows, which featured molded African motifs in bright colors. The upper levels are handsomely divided into twelve bays on the south side and nine on the east. The theater, which was the centerpiece of the community cultural center, had a special entrance that featured a Moorish design. The interior of the lavish theater was decorated with an African motif of spears, monkeys, and sphinxes, celebrating African heritage.

A very large building with 48,000 square feet, the Walker Building's primary function was to provide space for the operation, manufacturing, and distribution of the Walker Manufacturing Company. However, it also housed a beauty school, barber and beauty shops, a pharmacy, a restaurant, meeting rooms, a ballroom, and the splendid Walker Theatre. It became the hub of activity for the African-American community in Indianapolis. Some described the building as having a city within its walls.

Sarah Breedlove Walker, the force behind the creation of the Walker Manufacturing Company, who later in life was known as Madam C. J. Walker, was born in 1867 in a one-room cabin in Louisiana to sharecropper parents who were former slaves. When Sarah was old enough to go to school, the educational reforms for African Americans that had been made during the period of Reconstruction following the Civil War were being dismantled in Louisiana, and there was no public school

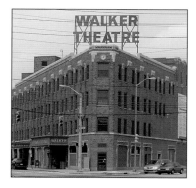

# Madam C. J. Walker Building

617 Indiana Avenue
Indianapolis, IN 46202
317-236-2099
*www.walkertheatre.org*
NRIS No. 80000062
NHL

**DATE BUILT**
1927

**ARCHITECT**
Rubush and Hunter

**ORIGINAL OWNER**
Walker Manufacturing Company

**SIGNIFICANCE**
As the center of the beauty industry established by Madam C. J. Walker, the Madam C. J. Walker Building served from 1927 to 1978 as the company's national headquarters, its manufacturing site, and as a cultural center. At the height of her career, Madam C. J. Walker was one of the most successful women entrepreneurs in the country and provided jobs for thousands of women.

that would admit her. She claimed to have had only three months of formal education. By the time she was seven both of her parents had died and she went to live with a married sister whose husband had a violent temper and considered his sister-in-law an unwanted burden. Like many other young African-American girls of her time, Sarah began to work, bending over boiling tubs of hot water, washing clothes.

Economic hardship, deadly yellow fever epidemics, and frequent violence against African Americans, including lynchings, were all part of Sarah's early experiences. But even at a young age she showed determination and a hopefulness about life, and refused to let the fear in the African-American community and the wretchedness of her situation defeat her. She dreamed of another life where she would live among beautiful things.

Sarah married Moses McWilliams when she was fourteen years old and became a mother at seventeen. She had only one child, a daughter named A'Lelia. Moses died two years later, when Sarah was only nineteen. Eager to leave the South in search of better opportunities, Sarah and A'Lelia moved to St. Louis where for the next seventeen years Sarah worked as a washerwoman. She became active in the St. Paul African Methodist Episcopal Church, began attending a night school, and participated in church clubs. Through various church groups she had contact with educated, prosperous African Americans, and through her participation in Sunday School and church women's organizations, she began to gain confidence in her organizing skills. Her goal was to find an alternative to the harsh, backbreaking drudgery of being a washerwoman, and she yearned for a different life for her daughter.

In the mid-1890s, when Walker was around thirty years old, her hair began to fall out. Many African-American women had this problem, which today is generally attributed to infrequent washing, perhaps only a few times a year, and to a poor diet. Sarah began experimenting with existing hair care products but nothing helped. Ashamed of her appearance and desperate to find a cure for her balding, as she later recounted, she prayed to the Lord for guidance and then had a dream in which a man gave her instructions on what African and American ingredients to mix. She concocted a lotion, and to her surprise it worked. Her hair began to grow back. She then tried it out on some friends, who also had positive results.

Though Sarah's original intent was to seek a cure for herself, she soon went into business selling her scalp ointments and soap. The primary element of her products was a sulfur-based ingredient commonly used in many scalp medications of the period. Much of the success of her mixtures was related to her advice to shampoo regularly, massage the scalp, eat a nutritional diet, as well as use her product. In her marketing, the way she packaged and advertised her products, she capitalized on what she said were the magical healing powers of her African ingredients and her claim that the formula was revealed to her by divine intervention.

With renewed motivation, Sarah moved to Denver in 1905, where one of her sisters lived and where she believed she could make a new start in life. She worked as a cook in a boardinghouse while she worked on perfecting her products. In 1906 she married Charles J. Walker and soon began to use the title of "Madam." In this period white people called African-American adults by their first names and reserved the titles of Mr. and Mrs. for whites. By using Madam, Sarah Walker claimed not only a title of respect that the French used for married women, but also one that would provide a stylish flair for marketing her products. Walker's husband was a newsman and his experience in mail order and advertising added a new dimension to her business. Her first sales efforts were door-to-door solicitations in which she

*In this 1912 photograph Madam C. J. Walker sits in the driver's seat with her niece to her right. In the backseat are Alice Kelly (behind Walker), the forewoman of the Walker factory, and Walker's secretary, Lucy Flint. Walker traveled often, so it is not surprising that she enthusiastically adopted the relatively new method of transportation called the automobile.*

demonstrated her products and the "Walker Method" of shampooing with her Vegetable Shampoo, applying the Wonderful Hair Grower, brushing vigorously, and using a heated iron comb for special hairdressing techniques.

Much of Walker's business success came from the fact that she recognized the close connection between physical appearance and prosperity. Specifically, she saw good grooming and hair care as an indicator of class and upward mobility. Although some critics accused her of advertising products to straighten hair, Walker never used the term "hair straightener" in her ads, but instead considered herself a hair culturist, encouraging healthy and attractive hair.

In the second full year of operation, Madam Walker's business expanded, and her income tripled. Over the next few years, however, she experienced increasing tension with her husband, who was less disciplined and ambitious than she and they soon divorced. She subsequently relied even more on her stylish daughter, A'Lelia, who was now in her twenties and had become a key partner in the business. While Walker went on promotional tours throughout the country, A'Lelia headed up the mail-order business.

*Faculty and the 1939 graduating class of the St. Louis Beauty School gather for a picture in front of the Madam Walker beauty school and supply store. The fame of the Walker supplies spread even to Europe, where the African-American entertainer Josephine Baker adopted the Walker System of hair care and styling.*

Madam C. J. Walker's beauty business made it possible for African-American women to enhance their physical appearance, and it created new job opportunities for them as hairdressers and as sales agents, known as "Walker Agents." Dressed in white shirtwaist blouses and long black skirts, the 5,000 Walker Agents scattered about the country in 1910 taught women to set up beauty shops in their homes and how to use Walker products. Since most of the job opportunities available to African-American women at this time were domestic positions, Walker provided a rare opportunity for African-American women to achieve a higher occupational status and better wages. Walker believed that one of the ways to gain access to American places of power was to be well groomed, and if African-American women looked more "acceptable" they could move into the mainstream of society and find new employment options. Walker's establishment of African-America women in business stretched from the president to the sales force, and according to her company's charter, the president would always be a woman.

The first Walker manufacturing headquarters opened in 1907 in Denver, with a second office established in 1908 in Pittsburgh. A'Lelia operated the Pittsburgh office and also ran a school to train door-to-door salespeople in the Walker Method. In 1910 Madam Walker sought to consolidate her operation in a more central location and decided to transfer the entire manufacturing operation to a new headquarters in Indianapolis, Indiana. In 1916 the business took another major step with the opening of the luxurious Walker Salon in Harlem, New York. A'Lelia presided over the lavish operation and developed ties with the business, social, and cultural leaders of Harlem.

The New York salon and Madam Walker's increasing contact with the African-American leaders of the day, such as the great African-American educators Booker T. Washington and Mary McLeod Bethune, as well as her participation and support of national African-American organizations, prompted her desire for a home in New York, which she considered the black capital of the world. She chose an affluent neighborhood along the Hudson River, commissioned Vertner Woodson Tandy, one of New York's most renowned African-American architects, to design the house, and spared no expense to create a magnificent home for herself.

*This tin container with a portrait of Madam Walker on the lid provided the decorative packaging for Walker's Wonderful Hair Grower, an ointment consisting of petroleum jelly and a medicinal sulfur.*

*Delegates to the national conventions of Madam C. J. Walker's agents wore official badges featuring an elaborately framed portrait of Madam Walker. During the conventions, Walker instilled in the agents her commitment to supporting black philanthropic work by giving a cash prize to the local organization of agents that had been the most generous to the African-American community.*

*In this 1915 photograph of the interior of a Walker Salon, several women beauticians work on the hair of their customers. In addition to selling products, the Madam C. J. Walker agent-operators also established parlors in their homes for giving scalp treatments and styling hair. All of the Walker agents signed contracts stating that they would use only Walker products and methods.*

When Walker moved into her elegant mansion in 1917, the Italian opera singer Enrico Caruso was among the first visitors, and he coined its name, "Villa Lewaro," by using letters from the name of A'Lelia Walker, the only child of Walker. With thirty-five rooms, including great halls, formal reception rooms, billiard room, and gymnasium as well as rear terraced steps leading to a swimming pool fed by a fountain, Villa Lewaro was Tandy's masterpiece. While some African Americans accused her of "undue extravagance," Madam C. J. Walker saw Villa Lewaro as a symbol of African-American accomplishment and as a reminder to young people of what a lone woman could accomplish.

Prior to her death in 1919, Madam C. J. Walker had the vision and plan for a new headquarters building in Indianapolis that would serve as a business headquarters and also as a cultural center for African Americans. In this period of segregation, African Americans were not allowed to go to white theaters, and thus in Indianapolis they had no access to the movies. Although Madam Walker died before the dream was realized, A'Lelia oversaw the fulfillment of her mother's design. In addition to being a corporate headquarters, a cosmetics manufacturing facility, and a sales-training facility for approximately 3,000 African-American women, the building included the first black-owned-and-operated theater building in the country. The Walker Theatre opened to a full house on December 26, 1927, and booked only top-quality entertainment, usually consisting of a feature film, a jazz band, and organ selections.

With the passage of fifty years, urban renewal, desegregation, and suburban settlement all had an effect on downtown Indianapolis. The Walker Building closed in 1978. The Madame Walker Urban Life Center, Inc., was created in 1979 as a nonprofit organization with the purpose of saving the Walker Building from demolition. As part of a major urban renewal effort in Indianapolis, the Walker Theatre opened in 1988. The United Negro College Fund and the Walker Eye Clinic, as well as a number of other offices and businesses, now occupy the building. In 1996, the Madame Walker Urban Life Center became the Madame Walker Theatre Center to more fully reflect the organization's mission of providing multi-cultural and educational opportunities and promoting the performing arts.

*At the 1924 convention of Walker agents, held at Walker's extravagant home, Villa Lewaro, the delegates gather on the various terraces around the reflecting pool. Built in 1917 by Madam Walker, this Italianate country home was decorated with oriental rugs, fine oil paintings, and a gold-plated piano.*

*Maggie Walker's Richmond, Virginia, home features decorative columns, an elaborate chandelier, and a grand piano. When the Walker family sold it to the National Park Service in 1979, the sale included all of the contents; thus the furnishings are all pieces originally owned by Walker.*

## BRANDYWINE MANOR

102 South First Avenue
Coatesville, PA 19320
610-384-2666
*www.graystonesociety.org/ brandywine.htm*
NHL

Unlike the self-made Madam C. J. Walker, many women business owners in the nineteenth and early twentieth centuries inherited their positions. Rebecca Lukens took over the Brandywine Ironworks in 1825 following the deaths of her father and husband. By careful management, she secured and maintained a significant market share creating one of the industry's major firms in the decades before the Civil War. She was the only women in this period to head a heavy industry that had interstate and international interests.

From her office in her home, called Brandywine Manor, she was able to oversee the iron works she owned and managed until 1854. Although called a manor, the two-and-a-half-story house resembles a typical farm house and has only three rooms on the first floor.

## HESTER E. SUYDAM BOARDING HOUSE

209 West River Street
Fromberg, MT 59029

From the time of the first towns in America, women have made a living managing boardinghouses. Since early notions of womanhood focused on women's place in the home, taking in a few boarders to pay rent was a natural extension of woman's role. Hester E. Suydam's boardinghouse in Fromberg, Montana, illustrates not only the growth of a small rural town, but also the ability of Suydam to build a profitable business. From its establishment in 1899, Fromberg quickly grew into a retail center for the surrounding area. Suydam recognized the need for temporary housing and moved from a nearby town in 1907 to build the boardinghouse, which has the outward appearance of a large single-family dwelling. The 1920 census notes that the occupants of the boardinghouse included a teacher, a sales clerk, a carpenter, a fireman, and miners.

## MAGGIE L. WALKER HOME

110 ½ East Leigh Street
Richmond, VA 23219
804-771-2017
*www.nps.gov/malw/home.htm*
NPS

Maggie Walker was the first woman in America to found and to head a bank. After teaching school for a few years she married a building contractor and had three children. Maggie Walker's interest in insurance began while she was a teenager and joined the Grand United Order of St. Luke, an African-American society that ensured care of its sick and proper burial of its members.

Over the years the Grand Order of St. Luke grew to include 1,500 chapters across the country, and Walker became executive secretary-treasurer. She led the effort in 1903 to establish the St. Luke Penny Savings Bank.

Walker's home in Richmond, Virginia, reflects her wealth and status in the community as well as her business and charitable interests. Built in 1883, the house was located in the center of Richmond's African-American business and social life at the turn of the century. The Walker family purchased the row house in 1904 and made a number of additions and alterations, expanding the house from nine to twenty-five rooms.

# Pewabic Pottery

## Detroit, Mich.

### Experimenting with Art Forms

As a nationally recognized potter who during the early twentieth century created remarkable iridescent glazes, Mary Chase Perry Stratton believed in innovation. She worked by the basic principle that "one never learns anything by copying others, but by constant experiments, one can arrive at something which is distinctly his own." Rooted in the arts and crafts movement that began in the late nineteenth century in England, Stratton founded her company, Pewabic Pottery, in 1903. The name Pewabic came from the Chippewa Indian word meaning "clay with a copper color," and recalled for Perry the town of her birth, Hancock, Michigan, the location of the Pewabic Copper Mine. At Pewabic Pottery, Stratton fostered the production of beautiful and functional objects that

*This photograph of Mary Chase Perry at twenty-eight (above), appeared in the February 1905 issue of* Keramic Studio, *a ceramics journal published in Syracuse, New York, the home of the New York State School of Clay-Working and Ceramics. From 1907, when Perry built Pewabic Pottery (right), to the present, the building has served as a studio and an exhibition gallery.*

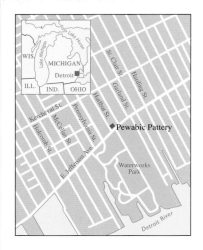

would be valued over the years. In 1907, the same year Pewabic Pottery's new ceramic studio was constructed, Stratton participated in the founding of Detroit's Society of Arts and Crafts. Many years later Stratton recalled that their goal was to avoid the ugliness of mass-produced, machine-made products.

In the twenty-first century, major art museums in the United States exhibit the work of women who excelled in America's art potteries at the turn of the nineteenth century. In addition to the work of Mary Stratton, many museums exhibit the pottery of Maria Nichols Storer, who in 1880 founded Cincinnati's Rookwood Pottery as well as Newcomb Pottery in New Orleans, which served as a training center for women in the decorative arts. However, one of the special aspects of Stratton's Pewabic Pottery is the fact that artists continue to produce handsome handmade pottery in the original building, much as they did in the past.

Mary Chase Perry, who was born in Michigan in 1867, exhibited a talent for art at a very early age. As a child she decorated eggshells, painted designs on fabric, and sold hand-painted Christmas cards. As a young woman she studied china painting and then clay modeling and sculpture. In her twenties she joined with three friends whom she had met at the Detroit Art Academy and opened a china-decorating studio. To harden the glazes they applied to the china, they placed the porcelain dishes into a special oven called a low-heat gasoline kiln.

In 1898, Perry entered into a partnership with Horace Caulkins, who had developed a new kiln for use in manufacturing china and producing porcelain for dentistry. His Revelation China Kiln, a small portable kerosene kiln that could fire at very high temperatures, proved to be an essential component in the creation of Pewabic pottery. The kiln had a hinged door and was lined with firebricks that allowed porcelain and ceramics to bake in a safer and cleaner manner than had been possible with high-heat kilns.

After realizing the potential of the Revelation Kiln, Perry began to experiment with clay and various glazes. Perry mastered the skills of using the potter's wheel and shaping pottery, but she also had an intense interest in the development of the clay glaze formulas and firing techniques. After studying technical books at the public library and ordering needed materials by mail, she weighed out ingredients and spent over a year testing numerous combinations for her clay and working to discover glazes that had exceptional textures and colors. In 1901 she attended three weeks of private instruction at the New York State School of Clay-Working and Ceramics, which had been established the previous year at Alfred University in northwest New York state. The school offered scientific, artistic, technical, and practical training for manufacturing all kinds of ceramic products, and its facilities included the first glass laboratory at any ceramic school in the world.

In 1903 Perry received her first commercial order, which was for a thousand dollars worth of bowls and lamp jars from Burley and Company, a Chicago company that specialized in all types of china and pottery. Burley and Company suggested that she adopt a trade name. It was then that Perry chose the name Pewabic. In 1903 the Burley and Company catalog noted that Pewabic Pottery was the result of an unprecedented process developed by Perry and described it as having glazes that "are soft and dull, yet lustrous and of a texture which is a delight to the touch."

During the next several years, Pewabic Pottery received many more commercial orders and expanded

*Mary Chase Perry demonstrates how to use a Revelation Kiln. Horace Caulkins, the inventor of this portable kiln and a partner in Pewabic Pottery, invited her to assist him in marketing the device, which she did quite successfully. The kiln achieved widespread use by china painters and by many of the country's leading art potters.*

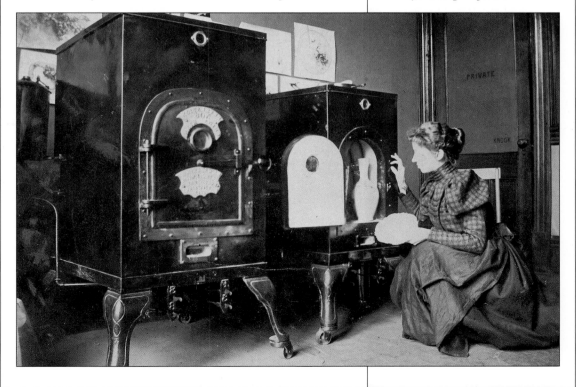

# Pewabic Pottery

10125 East Jefferson Avenue
Detroit, MI 48214
313-822-0954
*www.pewabic.com*
NRIS No. 71000430
NHL

**DATE BUILT**
1907

**ARCHITECT**
William Stratton

**SIGNIFICANCE**
Mary Chase Perry Stratton
founded Pewabic Pottery in
1903 with a focus on making
utilitarian as well as beautiful
hand-crafted objects. Stratton's
commitment was to quality
work and simple designs.
Working out of her Detroit studio, built in 1907, she achieved
a national reputation for vases,
bowls, and jars that are displayed in many museums, as
well as for tiles, which are featured in prominent buildings
throughout the United States,
including the National Shrine of
the Immaculate Conception in
Washington, D.C., and the
Nebraska State Capitol.

into the field of architectural tile, which became its best
known product. To fulfill large orders and to maintain
quality, Perry and her partner Caulkins adopted a management style that recognized their various skills. Perry
was the chief artist and the chemist for the glazes.
Caulkin focused on composition of the clay and was the
business manager. Her other partner, Joseph Herrick,
worked along with an assistant at the throwing wheel
following the designs created by Perry.

Perry's first interior tile installation was the surround
for the fireplace in her own home. Valuing the hand-
crafted aspect of tile, she emphasized simple design,
retained the rounded edges, and strove for exquisite
glazes. One of the first commercial orders for tile came
from the Griswold Hotel in Detroit, which wanted
Pewabic tile used in the decor of the bar. Soon there
were tile orders from outside of Detroit for fireplaces,
floors, fountains, and decorative panels, and trim,
including the Ford Corporation's early commission for
their administrative building in Omaha, Nebraska.

With this increase in demand came a need for more
space. Perry, in collaboration with her partner, decided
to build a new studio. Indicating a preference for
English architecture, they commissioned the architectural firm of Stratton and Baldwin, considered one of the
most influential in Detroit, to design the studio. William
B. Stratton, who was also a friend and a supporter of the
emerging arts and crafts movement, designed the studio
in the style of a rustic English inn.

Reminiscent of structures in the Cotswold area of
England, Pewabic Pottery was built in the Tudor revival
style. It had an exterior wooden framework with brick
filling in the spaces of the first floor and stucco filling in
the spaces on the second level. The building featured a
medium hip roof, meaning all four sides sloped down
from the peak, and two chimneys on the left side. The
interior had a large central room with high, two-story
ceilings, where the kilns for baking the pottery were
located. The lower level included a long, narrow room
for glazing and a smaller room for the throwing wheel.
The upper level had three large exhibition galleries with
fireplaces as well as three smaller offices or work areas.
One of the exhibit rooms was specially wired for dis-
playing twenty to thirty lamps, for Pewabic Pottery's
lamp making had become quite successful. The win-

dows, with panes of diamond-leaded glass, also reflected the Tudor style.

The opening celebration of the new Pewabic Pottery studio was an event made even more special by the presence of two distinguished guests: Charles Freer, the Detroit collector of Asian art, and Professor Arthur W. Dow of Columbia University in New York. Freer, the founder of the Freer Gallery in Washington, D.C., not only encouraged painters such as Whistler but also promoted the work of Perry. Freer's recommendations of Pewabic tile resulted in major contracts with prominent architects who used the tile for interior detail for churches, libraries, and commercial buildings. Professor Dow was equally impressed with the bowls and placed an order for plates and cups and saucers for a new dining room in the Household Arts Department of Teachers College, Columbia University.

In 1909 Perry's experiments produced her first iridescent glaze, which introduced a totally new look to

*On this page from Mary Chase Perry's daybook from November 1904, she made notations about pottery shapes and glazes, as well as the prices of each piece.*

the field of American pottery. Several years earlier Freer had urged Perry to experiment with the re-creation of the iridescent glazes of ancient Chinese ceramicware. Perry, who did not consider form to be as critical as her pottery's surface, excelled in the art of glaze chemistry. Critics applauded her shimmering hues that were ever-changing as the light around them varied. Perry liked to use more than one glaze, a technique that produced brilliant colors and unusual surface textures. Egyptian Blue, one of the most noted of the Pewabic glazes, possessed a special richness and strength of color. Though her formula and process has remained a secret, some collectors today believe that the iridescent quality comes from the combination of glaze composition and the process used in the cooling cycle. When Freer first saw one of Perry's iridescent pieces, he extolled its beauty. The three rooms on the second floor of Pewabic Pottery used for display were soon filled with samples of iridescent products. Many visitors came to view the exceptional pottery and to admire the glazes that captured the subtleties of light and suggested the glow of a sunrise or the mist of daybreak and in which colors flowed as in a painting.

*Mary Chase Perry's tile mosaic titled "Holy" appears over one of the arches in the Basilica of the National Shrine of the Immaculate Conception in Washington, D.C. During the building of this extraordinary church, Perry made many trips to Washington and conferred often with the architects and with Monsignor McKenna.*

In 1918 the Detroit Society of Arts and Crafts hosted the ninth annual convention of the American Federation of Arts, and Perry, Caulkins, and Stratton served on the planning committee. During the festivities of the convention, Perry and Stratton, after having been friends for three decades, announced their engagement and were married the next year.

Pewabic Pottery continued to gain national recognition with tile installations in prominent buildings in Detroit, Chicago, New York, and Houston. In Washington, D.C., Mary Chase Perry Stratton undertook her greatest challenge with the extensive use of Pewabic tiles in the Basilica of the National Shrine of the Immaculate Conception, a large Roman Catholic Church next to Catholic University. Perry provided tiles for mosaic ceilings and radiant iridescent tiles for the bands outlining the crypts and arches, and tile murals depicting the stations of the cross.

In 1921 the Art Institute of Chicago bestowed on Stratton the Frank G. Logan Medal in Applied Arts. Her highest honor came in 1947 when she received the Charles Fergus Binns Medal, awarded annually for the most outstanding work in American ceramics. Dr. S. R. Scholes, the Dean of the New York State College of Ceramics, wrote a letter recommending Stratton for this award. The letter stated: "Mrs. Stratton's total contribution to American Ceramic Art over a long period deserves recognition. Her Pewabic Pottery and her excellent development in decorative tile were outstanding at a time when comparatively few ceramic workers in this country were taking their medium seriously as an art expression. She was exhibiting experimental, unusual pots and tiles in 1907, many of which would still hold their own in 1947 national exhibitions." The letter of recommendation went on to note the artistic merit of her contributions to many public buildings and her great influence on the field of studio pottery.

In 1929 the Metropolitan Museum of Art in New York, in an exhibit of modern art, featured a fireplace designed by Perry in collaboration with the noted architect Eliel Saarinen. There were subsequent exhibits of Stratton's work at the New Jersey State Museum, the Corcoran Gallery in Washington, D.C., the Cincinnati Art Museum, and the Philadelphia Art Museum. But with the coming of the Depression, there was less money

*Perry received the Charles Fergus Binns Medal for Excellence in Ceramic Art in 1947. Binns, one of the founding members of the American Ceramic Society, was the founding director of the New York State School of Clay-Working and Ceramics, later renamed the New York State College of Ceramics at Alfred. Perry had studied ceramic chemistry under Binns in 1901.*

for architects to include elaborate tile installations in their plans. Pewabic Pottery, like other similar companies, experienced a decline in its contracts. And in 1939 Mary Chase Stratton lost one of her strongest supporters, her husband William, who died in a streetcar accident. However, Pewabic Pottery remained in operation and Stratton stayed at the helm until 1961, when she died at the age of ninety-four.

Soon after Mary Chase Perry Stratton's death, Michigan State University assumed ownership of the studio and used it for classrooms. In 1981 a group of potters in Detroit formed the nonprofit Pewabic Society, which uses the building for a combined program of instruction, exhibition, and ceramic production. The potters of the twenty-first century are still using the original cabinets, tables, clay-making machine, and dumbwaiter. Mary Roehm, the director of the Pewabic Society, noted in 1990 that the emphasis is still on func-

# Nampeyo, Renowned Potter

Nampeyo, a Hopi woman born in 1860 in one of the villages of the First Mesa in northeastern Arizona, led the way toward a resurgence of interest in Native American ceramics in the late nineteenth century. Archaeological excavations near her pueblo uncovered fragments of what had been long-unknown styles of ancient pottery. In her own pottery, Nampeyo adopted the forms and colors of these traditional designs. Many other potters in the surrounding area followed her lead, and there was soon a growing demand among collectors for pottery with traditional patterns and shapes.

Nampeyo and members of her family exhibited their pottery at the 1905 opening of the Grand Canyon's Hopi House, a store designed to showcase and sell Indian crafts. In 1910 she went to Chicago to demonstrate her pottery-making techniques at the United States Land and Irrigation Exposition. By the time of her death, in 1942, she was among the most respected Native American potters in the country.

*Because Nampeyo never signed her pieces, the task of identifying her work is difficult. Curators often refer to photographs of Nampeyo with her pottery to help authenticate her work.*

tionality and workmanship but that their charge "is to remain in the forefront of modern ceramics," a goal that she finds in keeping with Stratton's life and work.

Although more than one hundred years old, Pewabic Pottery studio continues to showcase ceramic work of noted potters as well as those at the beginning of their careers. Its mission remains consistent with the vision that Mary Stratton described when she stated: "It is not the aim of the pottery to become an enlarged, systematized commercial manufacturer in competition with others striving in the same way. Its idea has always been to solve progressively the various ceramic problems that arise in hope of working out the results and the artistic effects which may happily remain as memorials... or at least stamp this generation as one which brought about a revival of the ceramic arts and prove an inspiration to those who come after us."

Stratton, along with many women of the late nineteenth and early twentieth centuries, experimented with the application of old and neglected techniques and designs and excelled at incorporating them into new and innovative works in such fields as pottery, needlework, and architecture. With others in the arts and crafts movement, Stratton made beautiful and useful objects that were both profitable and artistic, and which have stood the test of time, increasing in value over the years.

*This picture of Perry at age ninety was the last official photograph of her taken at Pewabic Pottery. In her later years, Perry continued to teach and coordinate the workshops and exhibition facilities. After her death, one of her students, remembering the impact of her teaching, said, "I found my soul at the Pewabic Pottery."*

*Most of Pewabic Pottery's tiles were for architectural use, but collectors particularly value these commemorative designs. Some of the various limited-edition tiles made over the years include a decorative flower, a remembrance of a lecture series, a company's hundredth anniversary tile, a tile for the city of Huntington Woods, Michigan, and one for the Michigan Historical Society.*

## MARIE WEBSTER HOUSE

926 South Washington Street
Marion, IN 46953
765-664-9333
*www.mariewebster.net/
house.html*
NHL

Marie Webster, a master of artistic quilts, illustrated in her work the hand-crafted quality, simple lines, and artistic design of the arts and crafts movement. Webster's area of expertise and innovation was appliqued quilts, in which pieces of different fabrics are sewn onto a background fabric. She chose her colors carefully, often using several shades of one

*Marie Webster lived in this two-story clapboard house in Marion, Indiana, for forty years. Webster did all of her needlework in this house and used the sitting room to display quilts and quilt patterns to clients. The Quilters Hall of Fame now owns the house and is renovating it to use as its headquarters and museum.*

POPPY DESIGN
This is applied patchwork and therefore much more easily made than pieced work; very simple quilting gives prominence to the design

*With its elegant central design and vibrant colors, "Poppy" is one of Webster's most celebrated quilts. Her initials, MDW, and the date 1909 are quilted on the border.*

hue to give texture and a three-dimensional quality to her design. Webster's quilting career received a major boost with the January 1, 1911, issue of *Ladies Home Journal,* which featured full-color pictures of four of her quilt designs—"Pink Rose," "Snowflake," "Iris," and "Wind-blown Tulip."

Like Mary Chase Perry Stratton, Webster's role in the arts and crafts movement had an artistic as well as an entrepreneurial side. Webster revolutionized the production of quilts by forming the Practical Patchwork Company, which sold patterns, quilt kits, and even finished quilts. Her home in Marion, Indiana, was her headquarters, where she made her artistic quilts, wrote a book on the history of quilts, and established and operated her business, using closets to store her mail-order pattern kits. Her elegantly designed and sewn quilts are often on exhibit in the major art and textile museums in the country.

# 54 Tradd Street, Charleston Historic District

## Charleston, S.C.

### Preserving Historic Dwellings

**W**hile many cities value their status as large or modern, Charleston, South Carolina, has always treasured its history. Founded in 1670, Charleston gained a reputation before the Revolutionary War as a little London in the semi-tropical New World. When Fanny Kemble, the celebrated English actress, visited Charleston in 1838 she observed: "This city is the oldest I have yet seen in America. . . . The appearance of the city is highly picturesque, a word which can apply to none other of the American towns. . . and in one street you

*Susan Pringle Frost (above) was a Charlestonian to the core. She had a deep love for the southern city, and worked to ensure that it did not lose its old neighborhoods. In 1918 she took this photograph (right) of Tradd Street; Number 54, the three-story house at the center of the picture, became one of her early restoration projects.*

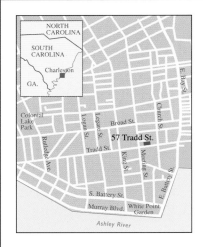

seem to be in an old English town, and in another in some continental city of France or Italy. This variety is extremely pleasing to the eye."

Located on a peninsula with the Cooper River on one side and the Ashley River on the other, historic Charleston constitutes a compact area of both grand and modest historic structures. Elizabeth O'Neill Verner, a noted twentieth-century Charleston artist, observed that "a library of historical data could never explain the charm of Charleston nor the passionate allegiance of her children." History and architecture are intertwined in Charleston. The city has its own unique style of homes, with the narrow ends of two-story houses facing the street, and porches along both levels of their longer sides. The city has retained whole historic neighborhoods with remarkably unaltered exteriors. Considering the importance of history to Charlestonians and the town's large number of well-preserved eighteenth- and nineteenth-century buildings, it is not surprising that Charleston has played an important role in the historic preservation movement, helping to pioneer many of the strategies that undergird the preservation of historic buildings.

Women were not only the early leaders but also the foot soldiers in numerous campaigns across the United States to preserve historic buildings from deterioration or demolition. Since nineteenth-century notions held that womanhood included being guardian of the home, protector of the nation's morality, and arbiter of taste, it seemed appropriate for women to lead the movement to save historic homes and communities from demolition and neglect. Ann Pamela Cunningham, the woman often heralded as the mother of the preservation movement, laid the foundation. The daughter of a wealthy South Carolina cotton planter, Cunningham charged into action in 1853 when she learned that developers were planning to purchase the neglected Mount Vernon, George Washington's plantation house outside of Alexandria, Virginia. The developers planned to tear it down to build a hotel. She mounted a spirited crusade that was successful in preserving President George Washington's home and its setting on the lovely hillside overlooking the Potomac River. The emphasis at this first stage of the historic preservation movement was on saving homes of distinguished national leaders. Historic preservation was very much intertwined with the creation of patriotic shrines.

Cunningham's leadership in the mid-nineteenth century established a national precedent for the role of women and of private citizens, not the government, in the preserving of individual structures associated with patriotic leaders and events. Following the example of the Mount Vernon Ladies' Association, many women's clubs, including chapters of the Daughters of the American Revolution, worked to preserve historic sites, many associated with military and patriotic leaders, such as the Yorktown battlefield and the Morris Mansion, which served as Washington's headquarters.

The woman who had a prominent role in the earliest stages of Charleston's historic preservation efforts was Susan Pringle Frost. Frost helped advance the historic preservation movement to its next step, that of saving whole neighborhoods of historic homes both grand and modest. A descendant of distinguished Charleston families, Frost spent her childhood in the Miles Brewton House, one of Charleston's grand mansions. However, the family's wealth had been wiped out by the Civil War, hurricanes, and family bankruptcy, and Frost, a single young women, had to find a means to support herself. Propelled into the workplace by the reversal of her family's fortunes, she found a stimulating life as a leader of the historic preservation movement. Frost landed her first job in 1901, working for eighteen months as a personal secretary to Bradford Gilbert, the prominent New York architect who had been commissioned to design the plan for the South Carolina Interstate and West Indian Exposition, which was to be held in Charleston. With increased interest in overseas trade, the leaders of Charleston hoped that the exposition would aid in their efforts toward economic revival. Working for the exposition provided Frost with an invaluable introduction to the fields of architecture and design as well as boosting her confidence in her workplace skills.

After the exposition ended, Frost studied shorthand and typing and then applied for a position as stenographer for the United States District Court, a position that she held for sixteen years. While working for the court she became a champion of women's rights, an advocate of social reform, and an investor in real estate. Using some of her meager savings from her stenographic job,

## 54 Tradd Street, Charleston Historic District

54 Tradd Street
Charleston, SC 29401
843-722-4630
*www.preservationsociety.org*
*www.historiccharleston.org*
*www.cr.nps.gov/nr/travel/Charleston*
NRIS No. 78002497
NHL

**DATE BUILT**
About 1740

**ORIGINAL OWNER**
William Vanderhorst

**SIGNIFICANCE**
Charleston, South Carolina, was the most prosperous eighteenth-century city south of Philadelphia. Many of the city's oldest streets became slums in the later part of the nineteenth century. The three-story house at 54 Tradd Street was one of the first purchases of Susan Pringle Frost, who was at the forefront of efforts to save the architectural treasures of whole neighborhoods in the core of the old city. Built around 1740 by William Vanderhorst, it is among the first single houses constructed in Charleston and was home to a number of distinguished individuals. In 1931 Charleston became the first city in the United States to designate an area as a historic district.

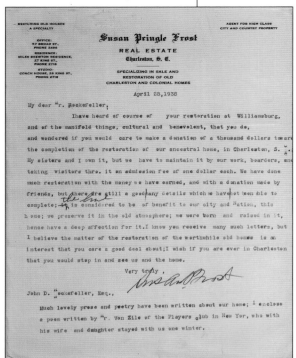

In 1938 Susan Frost wrote to John D. Rockefeller, the patron of the restoration of Williamsburg, Virginia, requesting financial assistance for the maintenance of the Miles Brewton House, which was her family's home. Her company letter-head lists her office on Broad Street, her residence as the Miles Brewton House, and her specialty as "restoring old houses."

she began her lifelong passion of buying and selling historic houses.

Frost's work in real estate provided a way to make money, while at the same time helping to preserve Charleston's architectural heritage. In July 1909 Susan Pringle Frost, who was then thirty-six years old, made her first purchases. They were two modest, dilapidated, pre–Revolutionary War houses located on a dirt road in the oldest part of Charleston, near the marshlands on the tip of the peninsula. Additional purchases followed, and in 1918 Pringle resigned her court stenographer job and opened her own real estate office. She became the first woman to join the recently formed Charleston Real Estate Exchange, an organization established to coordinate the work and practices of realtors in the city.

Frost devoted her life to urban initiatives with the goal of preserving the area at the core of the historic city. In some respects Frost seemed to value historic Charleston more for its sense of place and heritage than for its distinctive architecture, although she certainly appreciated the details of its structures. This distinction is best understood by recognizing that one of Frost's favorite words was "dwelling." Her family's roots and fond associations were attached to an area of her city that had become a rat-infested eyesore.

Frost's plan for rehabilitating the historic district involved buying and reconditioning old houses, repairing and painting as well as adding fine mantles and ironwork. The next step was to resell them to residents willing to work to create a new community in the old city. Frost had become a collector of artifacts from houses that were being torn down, and excelled in recycling these treasures by using them to help upgrade the houses she had purchased. One of the workmen on whom she relied was Thomas Pinckney, a skilled African-American craftsman who specialized in hand-carved woodwork. Pinckney had worked on a number of buildings in the historic area, including the home of Susan Frost's cousin, Ernest Pringle. Frost prepared the drawings for the renovations, and Pinckney built according to her specifications. Pinckney, described as "Sue's right-hand man," carved the doors, mantels, stairs, and moldings that gave Frost's restorations the charm and look that facilitated their resale. She also lobbied the city to pave the streets, an improvement that increased the value of her investments while improving sanitation in the area.

Frost called her strategy of investment "pyramiding," because she began with a small initial investment that expanded to a broad base. This approach involved taking one house at a time and restoring its beauty, then finding a buyer who appreciated the historic home and was willing to live in it. Frost's goal was to restore the historic neighborhood to the genteel residents who had previously lived there. However, this plan necessitated turning out the poor African Americans who were tenants in the run-down houses. Frost, anticipating criticism, went on record saying that her problem was with the owners of the decaying historic buildings and not with the African-American renters. Her situation reflects a tension that continues to confront the preservation movement: the restoration of blighted neighborhoods invariably means the displacement of the poor who have

*A delegation from the Congressional Union, which in 1917 became the National Woman's Party, gathers in 1915 at Frost's antebellum home at 4 Logan Street. The meeting was part of a state campaign to gain support for the woman's suffrage amendment.*

been living there. In recent years, there has often been a conscious effort to include a low-income housing component in preservation initiatives.

Not willing to rely only on her individual real estate efforts to save Charleston's historic houses, Frost organized the Society for the Preservation of Old Dwellings in 1920 with the express purpose of saving the Joseph Manigault house, which was slated for demolition. This 1803 three-story brick mansion had been designed by one of Charleston's early architects, Gabriel Manigault, and was considered by many to be an architectural gem. The Society for the Preservation of Old Dwellings was the first grass-roots historic preservation organization in America. The thirty-two original members adopted as their mission the goal of saving structures of historic and aesthetic distinction. Many years of perseverance went into ensuring the preservation of the Manigault House. Today it is among the premier house museums in Charleston. The Society, which saved the house from destruction, has changed its name to the Preservation Society of Charleston but continues its work toward the goals established by Frost.

Frost's vision of preserving entire streets and whole historic neighborhoods contributed to the concept of

*This postcard of a typical Charleston home proclaims Charleston as "America's Most Historic City." The narrow ends of many single-family houses in the historic area face the street. This creative response to scarce space allows more houses to line the street. Double-story side porches extend the length of the house to catch the sea breezes.*

C.T. 14—Typical Charleston Home, Charleston, S. C.
"America's Most Historic City"

establishing a historic district. Always keen to find new strategies, Frost was among the historic preservation leaders in Charleston who first considered the use of local government authority to preserve a city's architectural heritage. Her first tactic focused on exploring whether there could be a city ordinance to prohibit the removal of old ironwork and woodwork from Charleston. The sale of ironwork, mantels, and moldings by property owners had become widespread in the 1920s. Owners sought to make money by selling the trim from their houses, often to northerners who recognized the value of these architectural details for enhancing their own projects.

While the effort to prohibit the sale of architectural artifacts proved unsuccessful, Frost, along with a growing group of preservationists in Charleston, pursued the goal of implementing systematic urban planning through the use of zoning. This led in 1929 to the establishment of a Special Committee on Zoning, with the president of the Society for the Preservation of Old Dwellings chairing the committee. By 1931 the city council had taken on the project and that year adopted a zoning ordinance that gave the city authority to protect historic buildings and establish architectural standards for the construction of new buildings in the designated historic district. Although the boundaries of the historic district included less than 150 acres in the southeastern corner of Charleston, the zoning ordinance for a historic district set a national precedent. While zoning was beginning to be used in some cities for such purposes as protecting air quality and public health, this was the first-ever ordinance for a local historic district adopted in the United States. It put some significant regulatory teeth into the preservation movement.

Frost was one of the first in Charleston to champion the cause of historic preservation, but the movement gained followers, and new leaders emerged in the preservation movement. Laura Bragg, who in 1920 became the director of the Charleston Museum, recognized the connections between the museum world and historic preservation, and used her influence to preserve Charleston's historic buildings. Municipal officials oversaw not only the new historic preservation zoning ordinance, but also secured funding for the restoration of the Dock Street Theatre.

*Charleston's Manigault House, built in 1803 by a rice planter, is a grand three-story brick townhouse in the Federal style. The house is often called the Huguenot House because the Manigaults were descended from French Huguenots who came to America to escape persecution in Europe.*

During the 1920s and 30s, Charleston experienced a cultural renewal, called the Charleston Renaissance, in which artists, poets, novelists, and musicians expressed a profound appreciation for the uniqueness of Charleston's heritage, much of which was exemplified in its architecture. In 1947, with the establishment of the Historic Charleston Foundation, the preservation movement in Charleston was again in the forefront of the national movement. This time another woman, Frances Edmunds, was instrumental in the adoption of a new and effective strategy. Based on the creation of a "revolving fund" that could be used to provide financial assistance in the preservation of threatened historic buildings, Edmunds led the foundation in its work to preserve the city's historic architecture and to provide aid for the renovation of properties that could then be put to constructive use. Edmunds, like Frost, understood Charleston was a living city in which most of the historic buildings would continue to function as homes, offices, and stores rather than being frozen in time as historic house museums.

Despite Susan Pringle Frost's significant role in the initial stages of the historic preservation movement in Charleston, there are no markers recognizing her accomplishments. Most Charlestonians do not know anything about her. Yet the many historic dwellings that she helped to preserve serve as monuments to her life. Hundreds of thousands of people visit the historic district each year to see the treasurers of its acclaimed architecture. Tourism has become an anchor in the economy of Charleston, and guidebooks extol Charleston for having historic neighborhoods where one can easily stroll the streets, observe up close the splendor of its architecture, and gain a sense of the cultural heritage of one of America's unique and most beautiful cities. When Frost began her individual preservation efforts in 1909, she understood the value of preserving entire historic neighborhoods. This principle is today a cornerstone of the preservation movement.

*The central entrance hall in the Manigault House has a sweeping staircase leading to the second floor. The grace and elegance of the house reflects the lifestyle of its owner, who sat in the state legislature and was a trustee of the College of Charleston.*

## FREDERICK DOUGLASS NATIONAL HISTORIC SITE (CEDAR HILL)

1411 W Street, SE
Washington, DC 20020
202-426-5961
NPS

For twenty years Frederick Douglass, an abolitionist, writer, orator, and one of the most important African-American leaders of the nineteenth century, lived at Cedar Hill, an imposing Victorian home with a magnificent view over the Anacostia River of the nation's capitol. Born a slave, he became an advisor to President Lincoln and later the Recorder of Deeds for the District of Columbia.

After Frederick Douglass's death in 1895, his wife, Helen Douglass, worked to protect the handsome home on the hilltop as a memorial to him. However, when Helen died, the Historical Association that she had formed to ensure the preservation of Cedar Hill was unable to pay off the mortgage. As they did with Mount Vernon, it was women who came to the rescue. The National Association of Colored Women (NACW), established in 1896, had as its primary goals the establishment of schools and health facilities and the advancement of the cause of suffrage and civil rights for African Americans. In 1916 the NACW committed itself to saving Cedar Hill and successfully raised the necessary

*Houses such as this one in the French Quarter of New Orleans open onto the sidewalk and have balconies with decorative iron railings and trim. The historic district includes ninety blocks with more than 2,000 buildings, many dating from the colonial period.*

funds. The NACW maintained the home until 1988, when it became the Frederick Douglass National Historic Site, a unit of the National Park Service.

## VIEUX CARRÉ HISTORIC DISTRICT (FRENCH QUARTER)

New Orleans, LA 70116
NHL

Elizabeth Thomas Werlein spearheaded the New Orleans preservation movement. Born in 1883 in Michigan, Werlein was smart, stylish, and rich. In 1930 Werlein founded the Vieux Carré Property Owners Association and became its first president. Advocating stricter building codes, using the press to win public support, gaining cooperation from city officials, and nurturing a desire to preserve a local as well as national heritage, Werlein oversaw a major shift as the long-neglected French Quarter became a place of beauty and pride. Soon after the establishment in 1931 of the first local historic district, in Charleston, South Carolina, the French Quarter in New Orleans became in 1936 the second local historic district. When she died in 1946, the New Orleans *Times-Picayune* proclaimed that the vigor of her leadership and the breadth of her logic had been indispensable in the movement to retain the distinctive architectural character of the Vieux Carré.

## MOUNT VERNON
Alexandria, VA 22121
703-780-2000
*www.mountvernon.org*
NHL

Since neither the federal government nor the state of Virginia were taking steps in the early 1850s to prevent developers from demolishing Mount Vernon, Ann Pamela Cunningham spearheaded a successful private effort to save the historic home. Facing the Potomac River, this two-and-a-half-story wooden house was built in the Georgian style, which was popular in the eighteenth century and is characterized by a symmetrical exterior with a columned portico. As the main house of a large plantation, Mount Vernon was an impressive residence, but more than that, it was a house filled with historical significance as the home where George Washington had lived when he served as commander in chief of the Revolutionary forces and as the first President of the United States.

When the Mount Vernon Ladies' Association took possession of the property in 1860, an enormous amount of money was still needed for repairs, and the country was headed for a Civil War. But against great odds, Cunningham's astute strategies paid off and in 1867, she moved to Mount Vernon as the resident director, a position that she held until 1873. Mount Vernon today is still owned and operated by the Mount Vernon Ladies' Association.

*Ann Pamela Cunningham and the Vice-Regents of the Mount Vernon Ladies' Association pose in front of Mount Vernon in 1873. The Mount Vernon Ladies' Association continues today as a non-profit organization dedicated to the preservation of George Washington's home. Cunningham's meager beginnings in 1858 have evolved into a major undertaking, employing about 150 people.*

# Chronology

**About 1300**

Rise of Pueblo villages and culture

**1492**

Native Americans have first contact with Europeans

**1607**

English establish first settlement at Jamestown

**1619**

First enslaved Africans arrive in Virginia

**1648**

Margaret Brent demands a vote in Maryland's assembly

**1774**

Ann Lee establishes the United Society of Believers in Christ's Second Appearing, called Shakers

**1776**

Declaration of Independence is signed

**1790s**

First women's charitable and reform societies formed

**1804**

Sacajawea becomes an interpreter for the Lewis and Clark expedition

**1820s and 30s**

Evangelical revivals encourage woman's reform activities

**1821**

Emma Willard opens Troy Female Seminary

**1832**

Prudence Crandall admits African-American student to her girls school in Canterbury, Connecticut

**1837**

Boott Cotton Mill in Lowell, Massachusetts, builds a boardinghouse for its women workers

**1838**

Oberlin College accepts women and becomes the country's first co-educational college

**1848**

Seneca Falls women's rights convention

**1856**

Charter of the Mount Vernon Ladies' Association of the Union

**1860s**

Medical schools for women open in Philadelphia, New York, and Chicago

**1865**

Opening of Vassar College, which offers courses parallel to those at men's colleges

**1869**

Founding of the American Woman Suffrage Association and the National Woman Suffrage Association

**1872**

Susan B. Anthony arrested for trying to vote

**1887**

Jane Addams founds Hull House, one of the nation's first settlement houses

**1884**

Bryn Mawr College founded, first women's college to offer graduate degrees

**1920**

Ratification of the Nineteenth Amendment, giving women the right to vote

**1947**

Historic Charleston Foundation formed

**1966**

Historic St. Mary's Commission established

**1981**

Pewabic Society formed

# Further Reading

## American Women's History

Cott, Nancy F., ed. *The Young Oxford History of Women in the United States,* 11 vols. New York: Oxford University Press, 1989.

Evans, Sara M. *Born for Liberty: A History of Women in America.* New York: Free Press, 1989.

Flexner, Eleanor and Ellen Fitzpatrick (contributor). *Century of Struggle.* Cambridge: Belknap Press, 1996.

Hine, Darleme Cark, Elsa Barley Brown, and Rosalyn Terborg-Penn, eds. *Black Women in America: An Historical Encyclopedia.* Bloomington: Indiana University Press, 1994.

## Taos Pueblo

Demos, John. *The Tried and the True: Native American Women Confronting Colonization.* New York: Oxford University Press, 1995.

Green, Rayna. *Women in American Indian Society.* New York: Chelsea House, 1991.

Nash, Gary B. *Women in American Indian Society.* Englewood Cliffs, N.J.: Prentice-Hall, 1974.

## St. John's Freehold

Bailyn, Bernard. *The Peopling of British North America: An Introduction.* New York: Vintage, 1986.

Berkin, Carol. *First Generations: Women in Colonial America.* New York: Hill and Wang, 1996.

Kamensky, Jane. *The Colonial Mosaic: American Women 1600–1760.* New York: Oxford University Press, 1995.

## Watervliet Shaker Historic District

Braude, Ann. *Women and American Religion.* New York: Oxford University Press, 2000.

Campion, Nardi Reeder. *Mother Ann Lee: Morning Star of the Shakers.* Hanover, N.H.: University Press of New England, 1990.

Nicoletta, Julie, Morgan, Bret, and Robert P. Emlen. *Architecture of the Shakers.* Woodstock, Vt.: Countryman, 2000.

Smith, Louise A. *Mary Baker Eddy.* New York: Chelsea House, 1991.

Stein, Stephen J. *The Shaker Experience in America: A History of the United Society of Believers.* New Haven: Yale University Press, 1994.

## Boardinghouse at Boott Cotton Mill

Dublin, Thomas. *Women at Work: The Transformation of Work and Community in Lowell, Massachusetts, 1826–1860.* New York: Columbia University Press, 1979.

Eisler, Benita, ed. *The Lowell Offering: Writings by New England Mill Women (1840–1845).* New York: Norton, 1997.

Goldberg, Michael. *Breaking New Ground: American Women 1800–1848.* New York: Oxford University Press, 1994.

## Women's Rights National Historical Park

DuBois, Ellen Carol. *Feminism and Suffrage: The Emergence of an Independent Women's Movement in America 1848–1869.* Ithaca, N.Y.: Cornell University Press, 1980.

Dubois, Ellen Carol, and Gerda Lerner, eds. *The Elizabeth Cady Stanton–Susan B. Anthony Reader: Correspondence, Writings, Speeches.* Boston: Northeastern University Press, 1992.

Goldberg, Michael. *Breaking New Ground: American Women 1800–1848.* New York: Oxford University Press, 1994.

Sigerman, Harriet. *An Unfinished Battle: American Women 1848–1865.* New York: Oxford University Press, 1994.

———. *Elizabeth Cady Stanton: The Right Is Ours.* New York: Oxford University Press, 2001.

Weisberg, Barbara. *Susan B. Anthony.* New York: Chelsea House, 1988.

## United Charities Building

Hewitt, Nancy A. *Women's Activism and Social Change: Rochester, New York, 1822–1872.* Ithaca, N.Y.: Cornell University Press, 1984.

Kittredge, Mary. *Jane Addams.* New York: Chelsea House, 1988.

Sklar, Kathryn Kish. *Florence Kelley and the Nation's Work.* New Haven: Yale University Press, 1995

Waugh, Joan. *Unsentimental Reformer: The Life of Josephine Shaw Lowell.* Cambridge: Harvard University Press, 1997.

## M. Carey Thomas Library

Horowitz, Helen Lefkowitz. *Alma Mater: Design and Experience in the Women's Colleges from Their Nineteenth-Century Beginnings to the 1930s.* New York: Knopf, 1984.

——— *The Power and Passion of M. Carey Thomas.* New York: Knopf, 1994.

Lutz, Alma. *Emma Willard: Pioneer Educator of American Women.* Boston: Beacon Press, 1964.

Solomon, Barbara Miller. *In the Company of Educated Women: A History of Women and Higher Education in America.* New Haven: Yale University Press, 1985.

## Asilomar Conference Center

Boutelle, Sara Holmes. *Julia Morgan, Architect.* New York: Abbeville Press, 1988.

Cole, Doris. *From Tipi To Skyscraper: A History of Women in Architecture.* Cambridge: MIT Press, 1978.

Grattan,Virginia L. *Mary Colter: Builder Upon the Red Earth.* Flagstaff, Ariz.: Northland Press, 1980.

James, Cary. *Julia Morgan.* New York: Chelsea House, 1990.

Torre, Susan, ed. *Women in American Architecture: A Historic and Contemporary Perspective.* New York: Whitney Library of Design, 1977.

## Madam C. J. Walker Building

Bundles, A'Lelia, *Madam C. J. Walker—Entrepreneur.* New York: Chelsea House, 1991.

———. *On Her Own Ground: The Life and Times of Madam C. J. Walker.* New York: Scribner, 2001.

Lowry, Beverly. *Her Dream of Dreams: The Rise and Triumph of Madam C. J. Walker.* New York: Knopf, 2003.

## Pewabic Pottery

Cohen, Daniel. "Modern Mosaic," *Historic Preservation,* (March/April 1990): 30–35, 78.

Kaplan, Wendy. *The Art That is Life: The Arts and Crafts Movement in America 1875–1920.* Boston: Little, Brown, 1987.

Webster, Marie D. *Quilts: Their Story and How to Make Them, Practical Patchwork,* Santa Barbara, Calif.: Espadana Press, 1990.

## Charleston Historic District

Bland, Sidney. *Preserving Charleston's Past, Shaping Its Future, The Life and Times of Susan Pringle Frost.* Columbia: University of South Carolina Press, 1999.

Weyeneth, Robert. *Historic Preservation for a Living City: Historic Charleston Foundation 1947–1997.* Columbia: University of South Carolina Press, 2000.

# Index

References to illustrations and their captions are in *italic*. References to maps are indicated by *m*.

Howland Institute (N.Y.), 82

*How The Other Half Lives* (book, Riis), 69

Huguenot House. *See* Manigault House

Hull House (Ill.), 76–7

Hunt, Jane, 61

Ida B. Wells-Barnett House (Ill.), 78

Immigrant families, *69*; and Lowell mills, *50*; and settlement house movement, 76; Stanton, Elizabeth Cady, and, 60–1

Indentured servants, 26, 30–1; *30*

Industrial revolution, in America, 48

Ingle, Richard, 27

International Church of the Foursquare Gospel, 46

"In the Emblem of the Heavenly Sphere" (Shaker drawing), *43*

Iroquois women, 20

Jacobi, Mary Putnam, 77

Johns Hopkins University (Md.), 84

Joseph Manigault house. *See* Manigault House (Huguenot House)

Kelley, Florence, 77

Kelly, Alice, *105*

Kemble, Fanny, 121

Kennedy, John Stewart, 70–71

*Keramic Studio* (journal), *111*

Kivas, 16–7, *19*

Knife River Indian Villages National Historic Site (N.Dak.), 23

Labor movement, and women, 57, 77

*Ladies Home Journal* (magazine), 120

LeBrun, Pierre, 93

Lee, Ann, Mother: burial place of, *37m*, 45; description of, 36–7; as founder of first Shaker settlement, 36; imprisonment of, 38–9; as leader of Manchester Shaking Quakers, 38; legacy of, 46; marriage to Stanley, Abraham, 38; and "Shaking Quakers," 37–8; spiritual crusade of, 41–2; as spiritual Mother, 39; tenets of her religion, 39

Lewger, John, 25, 29, 31

"The Lily" (newspaper), *61*

Lincoln, Abraham, President, 130

Long, Sharon, 35

Low, Seth, 75

Lowell, Josephine Shaw, 68; and Charity Organization Society of New York City, *68*, 73; on coordination of charity work, 72; as first woman commissioner on State Board of Charities (N.Y.), 72–3; as guiding figure of United Charities Building, 75; memorial to, in Bryant Park, 75; philosophy of, 75; and Working Women's Society, 77

Lowell Female Labor Reform Association, 53

Lowell Historic Preservation Commission, 50

Lowell Mills (Mass.), 48; decline and revitalization of, 57; labels for bolts of cloth, *50*; labor movement and, 57; labor reform in, 53; management system of, 54–5; men in supervisory roles, 53; working conditions in, 51–3. *See also* Boardinghouse at Boott Cotton Mill, Lowell National Historic Park (Mass.)

Lowell National Historic Park (Mass.), 57

*Lowell Offering* (magazine), 53, 55–*56*; and creative writing in, 56

Lukens, Rebecca, 110

Lynchings, 78, 104

Lyon, Mary, 82

M. Carey Thomas Library (Pa.), 79–85, 87–*90*; architects for, *89*; architecture of, 79–82, 87; general plan of, *86*; Great Hall of, *81*, 90; renovation and reuse of, 89–90; Thomas, M. Carey, and, *86–88*

Madam C. J. Walker Building (Ind.), 102–9, *103m*; architecture of, 103; as hub of African-American community, 103; and nonprofit organization, Madame Walker Urban Life Center, Inc, 109; and United Negro College fund, 109; Walker, A'Lelia and, 108; Walker Eye Clinic in, 109; Walker Theater in, *102*; Walker Theatre Center in, 109; Walker Theatre in, 103, 108–9

Maggie L. Walker Home (Va.), *110*

Manchester Shaking Quaker community (Eng.), 38

Mandan Plains tribes, 23

Manigault, Gabriel, 126

Manigault House (Huguenot House), 126, *128–129*

Margaret Brent Award, American Bar Association, 26

Marie Webster House (Ind.), *120*

Marriage: colonial women and, 32; mill workers and, 51, 53; and Stratton, Mary Chase Perry, 117; Taos Pueblo women and, 19, 21; and Walker, C. J. Madam (Walker, Sarah Breedlove), 104

Martineau, Harriet, 55

Mary Baker Eddy House (Mass.), *47*

*Maryland Dove* (ship), 34

Massachusetts Institute of Technology (MIT) (Mass.), 94

Maybeck, Bernard, 93–5

McKenna, Monsignor, *116*

M'Clintock, Mary Ann, 61–4

M'Clintock House (N.Y.), 67; as part of Women's Rights National Park, 66

McPherson, Aimee Semple, 46–7; Angelus Temple of, 47

Merchants Exchange Building (Calif.), 99

Merrill Hall, Asilomar Conference Center (Calif.), 94, 99

Merrimack Manufacturing Company boardinghouse, 52

Merrimack River (Mass.), 49

Mesa Verde National Park (Colo.), 23

Metropolitan Museum of Art (N.Y.), 117

Middlebury College (Vt.), 91

Miles Brewton House (S.C.), 123

*Millennial Praises* (first Shaker hymnal), 41

Miriam Coffin Canaday Library, Bryn Mawr College (Pa.), 89

Monroe, Marilyn, 101

Morgan, Julia, 93; and arts and crafts movement, 94, 97; Asilomar Conference Center by, 96–9; at Ecole des Beaux-arts, 93, 95, 99–100; Fairmont Hotel, rebuilding by, 96; Greek Theater by, 95; Hearst Mining Building by, 95; Hearst San

# The National Register of Historic Places, National Park Service

The National Register of Historic Places is the official U.S. list of historic places worthy of preservation. Authorized under the National Historic Preservation Act of 1966, the National Register is part of a national program to coordinate and support public and private efforts to identify, evaluate, and protect America's historic and archeological resources. The National Register is administered by the National Park Service, which is part of the U.S. Department of the Interior.

Properties listed in the National Register include districts, sites, buildings, structures, and objects that are significant in U.S. history, architecture, archaeology, engineering, and culture. Places range from ancient Indian pueblos, to homes of writers or philanthropists, to bridges, to commercial districts. Among the tens of thousands of listings are: all historic areas in the National Park System; National Historic Landmarks; and properties nominated for their significance to communities, states, or the nation. The public can find information about these places on the web from the National Register Information System (NRIS) or request copies of documentation files.

For more information about the National Register of Historic Places, visit our Web site at www.cr.nps.gov/nr; phone 202-354-2213; fax 202-371-2229; e-mail nr_info@nps.gov; or write National Register of Historic Places, National Park Service, 1849 C Street, NW, Washington, DC 20240.

# Teaching with Historic Places

The Teaching with Historic Places program (TwHP) uses places listed in the National Register to enrich and enliven the study of history, social studies, geography and other subjects. Historic places have the power to make us more aware of our connection to the people and events that preceded us. It is possible to experience that "sense of place" whether or not site visits are possible. By actively investigating places and documentation about them, students can develop enthusiasm and curiosity while they enjoy a historian's sense of discovery and learn critical skills.

A series of lessons based on places around the country forms the cornerstone of the TwHP program. It includes Revolutionary and Civil War battlefields, presidential homes, churches that hosted Civil Rights meetings, places where women made history, and much more. Each lesson plan includes an activity that leads students to research the history and historic places in their own communities. TwHP lessons are free and available online, where they are indexed by state, historic theme, time period, and the National Standards for History.

For more information about the award-winning TwHP program or to acquire the lesson plans, visit the TwHP Web site at www.cr.nps.gov/nr/twhp; phone 202-354-2213; fax 202-371-2229; e-mail nr_twhp@nps.gov; or write Teaching with Historic Places, National Register of Historic Places, National Park Service, 1849 C Street, NW, Washington, DC 20240.

# Acknowledgments

I am indebted to my many friends, particularly those in the fields of women's history and public history, who provided suggestions to me as I was conceptualizing, researching, and writing this book. The excellent counsel and help that I received from the editors at Oxford University Press—Nancy Toff, editorial director, Children's and Young Adult Books, and Nancy Hirsch, project editor, Young Adult Reference Division—proved invaluable. Additionally my work depended greatly on frequent communication and assistance from my colleagues at the National Register: Carol D. Shull, Keeper of the National Register of Historic Places and Chief of the National Historic Landmarks Survey; Beth M. Boland, historian at the National Register of Historic Places and program manager of Teaching with Historic Places; and Alexis Abernathy, historian of the National Conference of State Historic Preservation Officers.

# Gilder Lehrman Institute of American History

Dedicated to collecting, preserving, interpreting, and promoting interest in the history of the United States, the Gilder Lehrman Institute of American History advances the study of history by offering public lectures, conferences, and exhibits; research fellowships for scholars to work in the Gilder Lehrman Collection and other archives of American history; summer seminars and enrichment programs for public, parochial, and independent school teachers; books, essays, journals, and educators' guides in American history; electronic media projects for students, teachers, scholars, and the general public; history-centered high schools and Saturday academies for New York City students; and prizes for the most outstanding books on Lincoln, the Civil War Era, Slavery, and Abolition. Founded in 1994 by businessmen and philanthropists Richard Gilder and Lewis E. Lehrman, the Institute's Advisory Board is made up of leading figures in the study and public presentation of American history. The Gilder Lehrman Institute may be contacted at:

19 W. 44th Street, Suite 500
New York, NY 10036-5902
646-366-9666
fax 646-366-9669
*http://www.gliah.uh.edu/index.cfm*

# Picture and Text Credits

## Pictures

A'Lelia Bundles/Walker Family Collection: 102 (top), 105, 106, 107, 109; American Textile History Museum: 50 (bottom), 55; Archives of the Basilica of the National Shrine of the Immaculate Conception, Washington, D.C. © All rights reserved: 116; From the Archives of the Seneca Falls Historical Society: 61; Arizona State Museum: 118; Bryn Mawr College: 79, 81 (top), 82, 83, 84, 86 (Photo by Frederick Hollyer), 88, 90 (Photograph by Broadbent Company); Julia Morgan Collection, California Polytechnic State University: 93, 99; California State Parks: 94, 95, 96, 97; The Charleston Museum: 121 (top), 128, 129; Chicago Historical Society: (title); Bob Thall for the Chicago Landmarks Commission: 78 (bottom); Columbia University Archives—Columbiana Library: 72; From *A History of the New York School of Social Work* by Elizabeth G. Meier © 1954 Columbia University Press. Reprinted with the permission of the publisher: 73; Denver Public Library: 14 (bottom), 20; Giraudon / Art Resource, NY: 38; Hancock Shaker Village: 43; © Hearst Castle, CA State Parks: 98, (Photo by Victoria Garagliano) 101; Historic St. Mary's City: 24 (bottom), 25, 27, 28, 31, 33, 35; *Indianapolis Star*: 102 (bottom); James Higgins Photography: 49, 54; Jim Steinhart of www.PlanetWare.com: 17, 19, 130; John H. Chafee Blackstone River Valley National Heritage Corridor Commission: 57; Library of Congress: 59, 62, 63, 66, 68 (bottom); Lynn Seldon: 110; Madame Walker Theatre Center: 104; Photo by Mark Thayer, The Mary Baker Eddy Library for the Betterment of Humanity: 47; Maryland State Archives, MSA SC 1480: 24 (top); Mt. Vernon Lady's Association: 131; Museum of the City of New York: "Kitchen of the Longshoreman Model Tenements, Brooklyn, N.Y." Mr. Alfred T. White, Print Archives, Gift of the Community Service Committee: 76, "Mrs. Robinson's Beauty Parlor," The Byron Collection 93.1.1.10837: 108, "Organized Charity," Jacob A. Riis Collection 90.13.3.10: 74, "Yard in Jersey Street," Jacob A. Riis Collection 90.13.2.55: 69; Museum of Indian Arts and Culture/ Laboratory of Anthropology, Museum of New Mexico. Photograph by Blair Clark: (18550/12 Ladder, early 20th century, Taos Pueblo) 16, (1892/11 Taos Black-on-White Ceramic Bowl ca. 1150–1250) 18; National Park Service, Lowell National Historical Park: 48, 50 (top), 52, 56, 51 (Houde/Jakszta Collection); *New York Daily Tribune*: 70; New York State Museum: 36, 39, 40, 42; McCormick Library of Special Collections, Northwestern Univ. Library: 14 (top); NPS: 23; Pewabic Pottery: 111, 113, 115, 117, 119, 120; Pine Mountain Settlement School: 78 (top); The Preservation Society of Charleston, Charleston, South Carolina: 121 (bottom), 125; The collection of the Prudence Crandall Museum (Connecticut Historical Commission): 91; The Schlesinger Library, Radcliffe Institute: 68 (top); The Rockefeller Archive Center: 124; Ronnie Lapinsky Sax: 64; Rosalind Webster Perry: 120; Shaker Heritage Society: 45; Shaker Village of Pleasant Hill: 41, 44; Collections of the SC Historical Society: 123; Sophia Smith Collection, Smith College: 58 (top); The Susan B. Anthony House: 67; Walter Cope Collection, University of Pennsylvania: 89; Photo by Will Faller, Vassar College: 92; Women's Rights National Historical Park: 58 (bottom), 60.

## Text

p. 30: Cott, Nancy F., ed. *Root of Bitterness: Documents of the Social History of American Women.* New York: E. P. Dutton, 1972, pp. 89–90.

p. 56: Eisler, Benita, ed. *The Lowell Offering: Writings by New England Mill Women (1840–1845).* New York: Norton, 1997, pp. 136–37.

p. 65: Flexner, Eleanor. *Century of Struggle: The Woman's Rights Movement in the United States.* New York: Atheneum, 1972, p.74.

p. 100: Morgan to Lucy and Pierre LeBrun, November 14, 1998, Special Collections Department. Robert E. Kennedy Library, California Polytechnic State University.

**Page Putnam Miller** is a Distinguished Visiting Lecturer in the history department at the University of South Carolina and the editor of *Reclaiming the Past: Landmarks of Women's History*. She was the executive director of the National Coordinating Committee for the Promotion of History from 1980 to 2000 and project director of the Women's History Landmark Project, a cooperative project of the National Park Service, the Organization of American Historians, and the National Coordinating Committee for the Promotion of History, from 1988 to 1993. She received the Women and Historic Preservation Award from the Third National Conference on Women and Historic Preservation.

**James Oliver Horton** is the Benjamin Banneker Professor of American Studies and History at George Washington University and director of the George Washington University Center for Public History and Public Culture. Horton has been honored with many awards for excellence in scholarship and teaching, as well as an appointment by President Clinton to serve on the Abraham Lincoln Bicentennial Commission. He has served as historical expert for First Lady Hillary Rodham Clinton on the White House Millennium Council; acting chair of the National Park System Advisory Board; Senior Advisor on Historical Interpretation and Public Education for the Director of the National Park Service; and historical advisor to museums throughout the world. In addition to consulting on film and video productions, he has himself been the subject of an episode in The History Channel series "Great Minds in American History." His numerous books include *Free People of Color: Inside the African American Community*, *The History of the African American People* (co-edited with Lois E. Horton), and *In Hope of Liberty: Culture, Protest, and Community Among Northern Free Blacks, 1700–1860* (coauthored with Lois E. Horton). In 2004, Horton will assume the presidency of the Organization of American Historians.